Charles Shwenn is a barrister with a broad commercial chancery practice. He has a particular interest in the law of costs and civil procedure, on which he regularly writes and advises.

# A Practical Guide to Non-Party Costs Orders

# A Practical Guide to Non-Party Costs Orders

Charles Shwenn, Barrister
Lincoln's Inn, LLB LLM (Exon)

Law Brief Publishing

The information in this book was believed to be correct at the time of writing. All content is for information purposes only and is not intended as legal advice. No liability is accepted by either the publisher or author for any errors or omissions (whether negligent or not) that it may contain. Professional advice should always be obtained before applying any information to particular circumstances.

Published 2021 by Law Brief Publishing, an imprint of Law Brief Publishing Ltd
30 The Parks
Minehead
Somerset
TA24 8BT

www.lawbriefpublishing.com

Paperback: 978-1-913715-56-4

*For my ever-supportive parents,*

*Chuck and Lynne.*

# PREFACE

It was a pleasure to be asked to write this book on a topic that will, it seems, only become more relevant as non-parties find new ways to become involved in the increasingly-complex process of litigation.

This is mostly a book about judicial discretion. It therefore could not, and does not purport to be, prescriptive. Its broad aims are to introduce and outline some of the concepts that have animated judicial thinking on the making of non-party costs orders. I have attempted to set out a framework for approaching the topic that I hope is user-friendly enough to qualify as a practical guide.

I am grateful to Tim Kevan and Garry Wright at Law Brief Publishing for their help and guidance on completing this text. My thanks also go to Bubbles Putnam, Rachel Collins, Samantha Cable and Jo Smith for their valuable assistance. Any mistakes and omissions are, of course, my responsibility. I have endeavoured to state the law correctly as of 1st December 2020.

Charles Shwenn
December 2020

# CONTENTS

# CHAPTER ONE
# THE BASIS OF THE JURISDICTION

The jurisdiction the court has to make a costs order against a non-party is ultimately concerned with ensuring that the costs of litigation are attributed fairly.

*The Origins of the Modern Jurisdiction*

The courts are afforded a wide degree of freedom in deciding what costs order to make. Rule 44.2(2) of the Civil Procedure Rules 1998 provides that:

> *44.2*
>
> …
>
> *(2) If the court decides to make an order about costs –*
>
> *(a) the general rule is that the unsuccessful party will be ordered to pay the costs of the successful party; but*
>
> *(b) the court may make a different order.*

The modern statutory authority for the making of non-party costs orders is section 51 of the Senior Courts Act 1981 which provides, in part:

> ***Section 51***
>
> *(1) Subject to the provisions of this or any other enactment and to rules of court, the costs of and incidental to all proceedings in—*
>
> *(a) the civil division of the Court of Appeal;*
>
> *(b) the High Court;*
>
> *(ba) the family court; and*

*(c) the county court,*

*shall be in the discretion of the court.*

...

*(3) The court shall have full power to determine by whom and to what extent the costs are to be paid.*

The Act[1] received royal assent on 28th July 1981. However, it was not until the 22nd May 1986, when the judgment of the House of Lords in *Aiden Shipping Co Ltd v Interbulk Ltd (The Vimeira) (No 2)* [1986] AC 965 was handed down, that it was confirmed that the court's discretion extended to persons who were not a party[2] to the substantive proceedings from which the costs arose.

In *Aiden Shipping*, Lord Goff found that there was no basis for implying a limitation on the court's discretion in section 51 of the 1981 Act that costs orders could only be made against parties to the litigation.[3] His lordship further suggested that the Rules Committee or appellate courts could respectively set limits to, and develop principles to guide the exercise of, such a discretion:

> *"I do not, for my part, foresee any injustice flowing from the abandonment of that implied limitation. Courts of first instance are, I believe, well capable of exercising their discretion under the statute in accordance with reason and justice. I cannot imagine any case arising in which some order for costs is made, in the exercise of the court's discretion, against some person who has no connection with the proceedings in question. If any problem arises, the Court of Appeal can lay down principles for the guidance of judges of first instance; or the Supreme Court Rule Committee can propose*

---

[1] Then referred to as the Supreme Court Act 1981.

[2] As to the definition of "party", see section 151(1) of the Senior Courts Act 1981.

[3] Reversing *Forbes-Smith v. Forbes-Smith* [1901] P. 258; *John Fairfax & Sons Pty. Ltd v. E. C. de Witt & Co. (Australia) Pty. Ltd* [1958] 1 QB 323.

*amendments to the Rules of the Supreme Court for the purpose of controlling the exercise of the statutory power vested in judges subject to rules of court."*[4]

<u>*The Discretion*</u>

In the event, the court's discretion has not been significantly curtailed by statutory intervention. In terms of guidance for judges of first instance, the increasing prevalence of applications for non-party costs orders has led to a body of caselaw intended to guide the exercise of the discretion.

Since *Aiden Shipping*, the courts have spoken of "accept[ing] the invitation of Lord Goff..."[5] and have attempted to lay down principles with broad application. However, the Supreme Court in *Travelers Insurance Co Ltd v XYZ* [2019] UKSC 48 recently summarised that:

*"the appellate courts have struggled to identify principles applicable across the board to the exercise of the jurisdiction to make a costs order against a non-party, save at the very highest level of generality".*[6]

The modern approach[7] has tended towards examining "in more granular detail, the principles which ought to apply to... distinct part[s] of the broad spectrum of non-parties".[8] It seems that courts will use what general principles there are as no more than a starting point,

---

[4] *Aiden Shipping Co Ltd v Interbulk Ltd (The Vimeira) (No 2)* [1986] AC 965, at 981 per Lord Goff.

[5] *Symphony Group Plc. v Hodgson* [1994] QB 179, at 192 per Balcombe LJ.

[6] *Travelers Insurance Co Ltd v XYZ* [2019] UKSC 48, at paragraph 28 per Lord Briggs.

[7] See *Barker v Confiance Ltd and others* [2020] EWCA Civ 111, *Money and another v Chapelgate Credit Opportunity Master Fund Ltd* [2020] EWCA Civ 246, *Travelers Insurance Co Ltd v XYZ* [2019] UKSC 48.

[8] *Travelers Insurance Co Ltd v XYZ* [2019] UKSC 48, at paragraph 30 per Lord Briggs.

incomplete without a more focused examination of any authorities applicable to the particular non-party under discussion and, of course, the individual facts of the case.

While the purpose of this text is to be of practical use in identifying the relevant principles, it must be remembered that the discretion afforded to judges of first instance remains broad. Pronouncements in subsequent caselaw serve as guidelines that may be departed from and have not be elevated to the status of rules.[9] The Court of Appeal has repeatedly warned that this jurisdiction is at risk of becoming "over-complicated by reference to authority"[10] and, echoing Lord Goff, "...since the decision involves an exercise of discretion, limited assistance is likely to be gained from the citation of other decisions at first instance..."[11]

<u>*Scope of this Text*</u>

The aim of this text is primarily to introduce the general and specific principles that have guided the exercise of the court's discretion. To that end, where possible, first-instance authorities have been avoided.

---

[9] *Petromec Inc. v Petroleo Brasileiro SA Petrobras* [2006] EWCA Civ 1038, at paragraph 11 per Longmore LJ; *Deutsche Bank A.G. v Sebastian Holdings Inc. and Alexander Vik* [2016] EWCA Civ 23, at paragraph 61 per Moore-Bick LJ.

[10] *Petromec Inc. v Petroleo Brasileiro SA Petrobras* [2006] EWCA Civ 1038, at paragraph 11 per Longmore LJ and paragraph 19 per Laws LJ. See also *Alan Phillips Associates Ltd v Dowling (t/as the Joseph Dowling Partnership) and others* [2007] EWCA Civ 64, at paragraph 31 per Moses LJ: *"There is now an abundance of authority on the absence of any need for abundant authority on the principles which should guide a judge as to whether to make a third party order for costs."*

[11] *Deutsche Bank A.G. v Sebastian Holdings Inc. and Alexander Vik* [2016] EWCA Civ 23, at paragraph 61 per Moore-Bick LJ. See *Barron MP and others v Collins MEP and another* [2018] All ER (D) 154 (Feb), at paragraph 79 on authorities for the proposition that the area should not become overburdened by authority.

It will also seek to provide guidance as to the procedure on the determination of an application for a non-party costs order.

Though section 51 of the 1981 Act permits (and the courts have occasionally ordered)[12] costs to be paid *in favour* of a non-party to litigation, there has been very little authority on the matter. This text therefore only concerns orders made against a non-party.

[12] See, for example, *Holden v Oyston* [2002] EWHC 819 (QB).

# PART ONE
# GENERAL PRINCIPLES

The Court of Appeal in *Deutsche Bank A.G. v Sebastian Holdings Inc. and Alexander Vik* [2016] EWCA Civ 23 said: "We think it important to emphasise that the only immutable principle is that the discretion must be exercised justly."[13] Unsurprisingly, there is no determinative test for when a particular person will be made subject to a non-party costs order.

Below the high threshold of immutability, however, the appellate courts have identified some general principles which, though not determinative, can serve as useful indicators for how the discretion may be exercised.

These principles can be divided into two categories. The first category concerns identifying types of non-parties who may be vulnerable to an order. The second category concerns additional principles of more discrete application that may be more or less relevant depending on the circumstances of the case.

---

13 *Deutsche Bank A.G. v Sebastian Holdings Inc. and Alexander Vik* [2016] EWCA Civ 23, at paragraph 62 per Moore-Bick LJ.

# CHAPTER TWO
# APPROACHES TO IDENTIFYING LIABLE NON-PARTIES

Lord Briggs in *Travelers Insurance Co Ltd v XYZ* [2019] UKSC 48 said:

> *"It is evident (from the Aiden Shipping case), and obviously right, that it is a pre-requisite for the making of a costs order against a non-party that the person sought to be made liable has some relevant connection with the proceedings in question."*[14]

The caselaw discloses at least three broad and potentially-overlapping approaches to assessing the non-parties' connection with proceedings: the most well-known and intelligible is where a non-party may be said to be "the real party" to the litigation; secondarily, and relatedly, where a non-party is "a real party" to the litigation; and finally, it seems, where a non-party may be said to have "unjustifiably intermeddled" with the litigation. These three categories may not be exhaustive and, as will be seen in the chapters that follow, provide only a starting point.

*"The Real Party"*

If a non-party can be said to be "the real party" to litigation, it will ordinarily be just to make a non-party costs order against them instead of the nominal party. The court here is concerned with ensuring that the costs burden falls on the correct person and preventing a person

[14] *Travelers Insurance Co Ltd v XYZ* [2019] UKSC 48, at paragraph 27 per Lord Briggs.

who is not a party to the proceedings escaping costs liability that is properly theirs.[15]

Though the concept had been applied before, in *Dymocks Franchise Systems (NSW) Pty Ltd v Todd* [2004] 1 WLR 2807, Lord Brown offered the following seminal definition of when the courts might view a person as "the real party":

> *"Where, however, the non-party not merely funds the proceedings but substantially also controls or at any rate is to benefit from them, justice will ordinarily require that, if the proceedings fail, he will pay the successful party's costs. The non-party in these cases is not so much facilitating access to justice by the party funded as himself gaining access to justice for his own purposes. He himself is 'the real party' to the litigation, a concept repeatedly invoked throughout the jurisprudence…"*[16]

*Dymocks* was a decision of the Privy Council, but the dictum of Lord Brown has been applied by courts consistently since being handed down. In *Deutsche Bank A.G. v Sebastian Holdings Inc. and Alexander Vik* [2016] EWCA Civ 23, the Court of Appeal confirmed that the decision "contains an authoritative statement of the modern law."[17] However, the court has also warned against treating this definition as completely comprehensive.

[15] See, for example, *Threlfall v ECD Insight Ltd and another* [2013] EWCA Civ 1444, at paragraph 13: "*…in deciding whether or not to make such an order, the court is not fettered by the legal realities. It is entitled to look to the economic realities. It is in this sense that many of the cases pose the question whether the non-party is 'the real party' in the case.*"

[16] *Dymocks Franchise Systems (NSW) Pty Ltd v Todd* [2004] 1 WLR 2807, at paragraph 25 per Lord Brown.

[17] *Deutsche Bank A.G. v Sebastian Holdings Inc. and Alexander Vik* [2016] EWCA Civ 23, at paragraph 61 per Moore-Bick LJ. But cf. paragraph 25 of that judgment where the definition in *Dymocks* appears to be treated as if it is conjunctive.

Specifically, if the party can still be described as "the real party" but the funding element is missing or at least cannot be resolved, it seems that this will not prevent a court from making an order on "the real party" basis. In *Petromec Inc. v Petroleo Brasileiro SA Petrobras* [2006] EWCA Civ 1038 the Court of Appeal warned:

> *"to read the words 'and funds' as imposing some requirement without the presence of which the discretion should not be exercised is to treat the words of Lord Brown as if they are a statute, which they most emphatically are not."*[18]

Additionally, it is worth noting that the motivation behind a non-party's involvement is an important consideration. This can be seen reflected in the caselaw on impropriety (as to which see Chapter 3), insurers in limits of cover cases (see Chapter 4) and company directors (see Chapter 7 and, specifically, the dictum of Millett LJ in *Metalloy Supplies Ltd v MA (UK) Ltd* [1997] 1 WLR 1613, at 1620).

The facts of *Deutsche Bank* offer a good illustration of "the real party" principle, as qualified by *Petromac*, in action.

The *Deutsche Bank* case is one of a long-running saga of litigation between the parties. Sebastian Holdings Inc. ('Sebastian') was a shell company incorporated in the Turks and Caicos Islands. It was used as a personal investment vehicle for Alexander Vik who was, at the relevant times, its sole shareholder and sole director.

The litigation related to Sebastian's accounts with Deutsche Bank for trading in foreign currencies, shares and financial products. In January 2009 Deutsche Bank began proceedings against Sebastian to recover approximately US$250m due principally in respect of amounts owed on the closing out of various trading positions. Sebastian brought a

---

[18] *Petromec Inc. v Petroleo Brasileiro SA Petrobras* [2006] EWCA Civ 1038.

counterclaim for approximately US$8bn in respect of the losses it alleged it had suffered as a result of the bank's breaches of contract in forcing it to close out certain open positions contrary to its wishes.

The matter came before Cooke J who gave judgment for the bank on its claim in the sum of US$243,023,089 and dismissed Sebastian's counterclaim. Sebastian was ordered to pay 85% of the bank's costs, which amounted to about £60m. Sebastian, which was said to have no assets, failed to pay anything in respect either of the judgment debt or the costs.

The bank then made an application for a non-party costs order against Mr Vik personally on the basis that:

> *"Mr Vik owned and controlled Sebastian, that he had directed the litigation on its behalf, that he had funded the litigation, or had made funds available to enable Sebastian to pursue it, that it had been conducted for his personal benefit and that therefore he was the 'real party' to the litigation."*[19]

In the first instance decision, which was upheld by the Court of Appeal, Cooke J could not decisively determine the issue of funding, however said:

> *"I do not need to reach this conclusion in relation to funding because, in my judgment, the other elements which I have found are more than sufficient to justify making an order for costs against Mr Vik personally.*
>
> ...
>
> *[Sebastian] SHI was Mr Vik's 'trading company' and his 'creature' company. Whilst it was treated by [Deutsche Bank] DBAG as a*

[19] *Deutsche Bank A.G. v Sebastian Holdings Inc. and Alexander Vik* [2016] EWCA Civ 23, at paragraph 3 per Moore-Bick LJ.

*corporate entity with legal personality... it was always seen as Mr Vik's company and DBAG looked to him in respect of all matters save for those trading decisions which he had entrusted to third party managers... the reality was that proceedings were pursued because it was Mr Vik who stood to gain or lose in the event of SHI's success or failure in the action. He was therefore the 'real party' to the dispute and to the action..."*[20]

As in this example, the concept of "the real party" has proven to be a relatively straightforward test to understand and apply. Some reflection of the concept of "the real party" is to be found in CPR 25.13(2)(f) which provides for a security for costs order to be made where "the claimant is acting as a nominal claimant" (see Chapter 3). Both jurisdictions are, of course, concerned with ensuring that an order for costs is ultimately met.

*"A Real Party"*

In *Dymocks*, having set out when a party may be considered "the real party", Lord Brown continued, citing Australian authority:

> *"Nor, indeed, is it necessary that the non-party be 'the only real party' to the litigation..., provided that he is 'a real party in ... very important and critical respects' (see Arundel Chiropractic Centre Pty Ltd v Deputy Comr of Taxation* [2001] HCA 26 at [37]*...)."*[21]

However, there is an important distinction to be made between a party who is "the real party" and one who is "a real party in very important

[20] *Deutsche Bank A.G. v Sebastian Holdings Inc. and Alexander Vik* [2014] EWHC 2073 (Comm), at paragraphs 92 and 85.

[21] *Dymocks Franchise Systems (NSW) Pty Ltd v Todd* [2004] 1 WLR 2807, at paragraph 25 per Lord Brown.

and critical respects". Both concern the connection the non-party has with the litigation and employ almost identical language, but the tests are different.

The standard required under the "the real party" approach is easily intelligible: it asks the court to evaluate the extent to which the non-party is, in substance but not form, the party nominally engaged in the proceedings. In contrast, the concept of "a real party in very important and critical respects" is not so clear. If more than one non-party could be liable for costs as "a real party", it leaves unanswered the standard expected for a non-party to qualify, in a way that the "the real party" test does not. As Lord Sumption recognised in *Travelers*: "non-parties may well have a more or less direct commercial interest in the outcome but do not thereby assume the risks associated with contested litigation."[22]

Leveson LJ considered the matter in *Flatman v Germany (Law Society intervening); Weddall v Barchester Health Care Ltd (Same intervening)* [2013] 1 WLR 2676, approving the judgment of Eady J below:

> *"Thus, as Eady J put it, if a funder is 'a real party' in the sense that he has an interest in the outcome of the litigation it may not matter that it would be inappropriate to describe that funder as 'the real party'. Eady J went on:*
>
> *'It may suffice, depending upon the circumstances, that the funder has something to gain alongside the nominal party…'"*[23]

[22] *Travelers Insurance Co Ltd v XYZ* [2019] UKSC 48, at paragraph 113 per Lord Sumption.

[23] *Flatman v Germany (Law Society intervening); Weddall v Barchester Health Care Ltd (Same intervening)* [2013] 1 WLR 2676, at 2686 per Leveson LJ.

What appears to be critical in cases where a non-party cannot be said to be "the real party" is a close examination of the nature of the interest he has in the litigation, which need not necessarily be financial.[24] The court will often be interested in why the non-party involved himself. From this, it can make a determination as to whether imposing liability is just; for example, and as will be seen later, it seems that certain motivations, such as bargain[25] and self-interest[26] will often result in a non-party costs order. Conversely, disinterested philanthropy will generally not.[27] More generally, Moore-Bick LJ in *Deutsche Bank* said this of a non-party under consideration:

> *"the critical factor in each case is the nature and degree of his connection with the proceedings, since that will ultimately determine whether it is appropriate to adopt a summary procedure of the kind envisaged in the authorities…"*[28]

The best practical understanding of the connection necessary under the "a real party" approach will be gained by examining its application, discussed more fully in Part 2. It is clearly a more flexible and open-ended approach than that of "the real party". This breadth ensures that, beyond the basic requirement to be just, the discretion afforded to judges in this jurisdiction remains largely unfettered.

---

[24] See, for instance, trade union cases (Chapter 10).

[25] See, for instance, commercial funding cases (Chapter 6) and particularly *ChapelGate Credit Opportunity Master Fund Limited v Money and others* [2020] EWCA Civ 246.

[26] See, for example, liability insurers in limits of cover cases (Chapter 4).

[27] See, for example, pure funder cases (Chapter 3).

[28] *Deutsche Bank A.G. v Sebastian Holdings Inc. and Alexander Vik* [2016] EWCA Civ 23, at paragraph 21 per Moore-Bick LJ.

*Unjustifiable Intermeddling*

In contrast to these approaches, where a non-party has "unjustifiably intermeddled" in litigation, the court may be receptive to a non-party costs application in respect of costs incurred by the intermeddling.

The concept of "unjustifiable intermeddling", has not been as widely employed as that of "the real party" or "a real party". Indeed, until recently, it was assumed that it applied only in the context of liability insurers (see Chapter 4). It seems, however, that the concept may have wider application.

In *Travelers*, a case concerning liability insurers, Lord Briggs cited with approval the case of *Murphy v Young & Co.'s Brewery Plc.* [1997] 1 WLR 1591, also an insurance case. In *Murphy*, Phillips LJ drew on the law of maintenance and champerty in the following terms:

> *"In Giles v. Thompson [1994] 1 AC 142, 164 Lord Mustill suggested that the current test of maintenance should ask the question whether:*
>
> *'there is wanton and officious intermeddling with the disputes of others in where the meddler has no interest whatever, and where the assistance he renders to one or the other party is without justification or excuse.'*
>
> *Where such a test is satisfied, I would expect the court to be receptive to an application under section 51 that the meddler pay any costs attributable to his intermeddling."*[29]

Though *Murphy* concerned insurers and the dictum of Phillips LJ had generally been applied in that context, his lordship certainly did not

[29] *Murphy v Young & Co.'s Brewery Plc.* [1997] 1 WLR 1591, at 1601 per Phillips LJ.

couch his analysis in terms restricting its application to insurance cases. In citing this dictum, however, Lord Briggs in *Travelers* confirmed that the intermeddling principle was "by no means limited to insurers".[30] It is clear from his concurring judgment that Lord Sumption adhered to the same view.[31]

Lord Briggs set out some definable features of the intermeddling principle in his leading judgment:

> *"This is a principle derived from the English law about maintenance and champerty.... Its starting assumption is that non-parties usually, although not invariably, have no legitimate interest in becoming involved in the litigation of others. It does not render involvement of any kind objectionable, but only involvement which is (in old-fashioned language) wanton and officious, for which the non-party cannot demonstrate some justification or excuse.*
>
> *This basis for the costs liability of the non-party does not necessarily depend upon showing that it has taken control of the litigation, or done anything approaching becoming the real defendant in it. Nor is there any fixed benchmark which will establish whether involvement has become a form of intermeddling. In every case the nature and extent of the non-party's involvement will have to be measured against the alleged justification or excuse for it.*
>
> *...If the non-party has not gone beyond the confines of those contractual obligations and attendant rights in framing its*

[30] *Travelers Insurance Co Ltd v XYZ* [2019] UKSC 48, at paragraph 36 per Lord Briggs.

[31] *Travelers Insurance Co Ltd v XYZ* [2019] UKSC 48, at paragraphs 113 – 117 per Lord Sumption.

> *involvement... liability as an intermeddler may be very hard to establish."*[32]

A broader analysis of the caselaw also shows that, although not necessarily using the same taxonomy, courts have been willing to apply[33] and make awards based on a non-party's unjustified intermeddling outside of the insurance context. One example is found in cases involving solicitors, who may be made subject to a non-party costs order if they act "outside of the role of a solicitor" in their conduct of a case, per *Tolstoy-Miloslavsky v Aldington* [1996] 1 WLR 736, as interpreted by *Myatt v National Coal Board and another (No 2)* [2007] 1 WLR 1559 and *Flatman v Germany (Law Society intervening); Weddall v Barchester Health Care Ltd (Same intervening)* [2013] 1 WLR 2676 at 2691 (as to which, see Chapter 9). Similarly, in *R (on the application of Laird) v Secretary of State for The Home Department* (QBD (Admin), Unreported, 8th April 2014 and 25th February 2016), Simler J indicated that a McKenzie friend who went beyond their proper role may have a non-party costs order made against them.

Nevertheless, whilst arguably a more straightforward approach, it must be recognised that the law on non-party meddlers outside of the insurance context is nascent; how it develops and is applied largely remains to be seen.[34]

---

32 *Travelers Insurance Co Ltd v XYZ* [2019] UKSC 48, at paragraphs 54 – 55 per Lord Briggs.

33 *Floods of Queensbury Ltd and another v Shand Construction Ltd and others* [2001] All ER (D) 153 (Apr); *In re RBS Rights Issue Litigation* [2017] 1 WLR 4635 (Note in this latter case at page 4658, Hildyard J appears to have elided the "a real party" and intermeddling tests).

34 *Ibid.* and cf. *Popely and another v Popely and others* [2020] EWHC 667 (Ch), at paragraph 11 per HHJ Hacon (sitting as a Deputy Judge of the High Court).

# CHAPTER THREE
# ADDITONAL PRINCIPLES

As has been seen, there are no immutable principles, applicable across the board, apart from that the discretion will be exercised "justly". Chapter 2 concerned broad categories of non-parties who may be vulnerable to a non-party costs order. In addition to these, the courts have identified some more specific principles which may affect the justness or otherwise of a non-party costs order in particular cases.

However, before considering those principles, it is worth recalling the warning of Mummery LJ in *Re Aurum Marketing Ltd (in liquidation)* [2000] 2 BCLC 645:

> *"There is guidance in the cases highlighting various factors relevant to the exercise of the discretion... but none of the authorities attempt to legislate for the exercise of the discretion. That must always depend on consideration of the actual circumstances of each case... It is wrong to treat the reported cases as providing a comprehensive checklist of factors which must be present in every case before the discretion can be exercised in a particular case. What may be sufficient to justify the exercise of the discretion in one case should not be treated as a necessary factor for the exercise of the discretion in a different case."*[35]

Though not exhaustive, therefore, the following principles emerge from the caselaw as potentially relevant:

1. Non-party costs orders are to be regarded as "exceptional";

---

[35] *Re Aurum Marketing Ltd (in liquidation)* [2000] 2 BCLC 645, at 650 per Mummery LJ.

2. The discretion will generally not be exercised against "pure funders";

3. Causation of the costs will be a relevant factor to consider;

4. A finding of impropriety is not necessary but may support the making of an order against a non-party;

5. A non-party costs application should not be used as a substitute for the pursuit of a related cause of action against the non-party in ordinary proceedings;

6. Security for costs may be relevant but is not determinative;

7. A failure to warn a non-party may be a relevant factor but is not decisive against liability.

*1. Exceptionality*

It has been said that non-party costs orders will be "exceptional". Discussion of exceptionality pervades the early caselaw on non-party costs orders but has become less focal in recent years. This is a welcome development as the concept offers little practical assistance in determining liability: the exceptionality of an order cannot be separated from the justness of an order, which is the real test.[36]

The question of the "exceptionality" of a non-party costs order can be traced back to the judgment of Lord Goff in *Aiden Shipping Co Ltd v Interbulk Ltd (The Vimeira) (No 2)* [1986] AC 965, where his lordship commented:

[36] *Deutsche Bank A.G. v Sebastian Holdings Inc. and Alexander Vik* [2016] EWCA Civ 23, at paragraph 62 per Moore-Bick LJ.

> *"In the vast majority of cases, it would no doubt be unjust to make an award of costs against a person who is not a party to the relevant proceedings. But, as the facts of the present case show, that is not always so."*[37]

This was interpreted by Balcombe LJ in the subsequent case of *Symphony Group Plc. v Hodgson* [1994] QB 179 who said:

> *"An order for the payment of costs by a non-party will always be exceptional: see per Lord Goff in Aiden Shipping Co Ltd v Interbulk Ltd (The Vimeira) (No 2) [1986] AC 965, 980F"*[38]

Cases in which the court will find it just to make a non-party costs order will *probably* be exceptional because it is unusual such an order will be justified on the facts. However, the exceptionality itself does not justify the order.

Regrettably, following the Court of Appeal's decision in *Symphony*, there has been a tendency for practitioners, courts and commentators to overemphasise the concept of "exceptionality" and treat the presence of some exceptional factor as something approaching a requirement[39] to the making a non-party costs order.

However, that approach appears to misread Lord Goff's dictum in *Aiden Shipping*. His lordship predicted that the court properly applying the operative principle[40] of "justice" will result in relatively few

---

37 *Aiden Shipping Co Ltd v Interbulk Ltd (The Vimeira) (No 2)* [1986] AC 965, at 980 per Lord Goff.

38 *Symphony Group Plc. v Hodgson* [1994] QB 179, at 192 per Balcombe LJ.

39 See, for example, *Dolphin Quays Developments Ltd v Mills and others* [2008] EWCA Civ 385, at paragraphs 71 – 75 per Lawrence Collins LJ.

40 See *Deutsche Bank A.G. v Sebastian Holdings Inc. and Alexander Vik* [2016] EWCA Civ 23, at paragraph 62 per Moore-Bick LJ.

cases being suitable for a non-party costs order. There was no intention to make the exceptionality of a case indicative of liability.

This is recognised implicitly by Lord Brown in *Dymocks Franchise Systems (NSW) Pty Ltd v Todd* [2004] 1 WLR 2807:

> *"Although costs orders against non-parties are to be regarded as 'exceptional', exceptional in this context means no more than outside the ordinary run of cases where parties pursue or defend claims for their own benefit and at their own expense..."*[41]

Lord Reed has more clearly expressed concern as to the influence of the concept of exceptionality in the recent decision of *Travelers Insurance Company Ltd v XYZ* [2019] UKSC 48:

> *"Lord Goff was not suggesting that exceptionality was a pre-condition. He was merely observing that cases in which it is just to make a non-party costs order form only a small proportion of the total... Indeed, exceptionality can scarcely be in itself an intelligible criterion for the making of a non-party costs order."*[42]

It is suggested that "exceptionality" itself is not a helpful basis upon which to base an application for a non-party costs order. It is not (and could not realistically be) a pre-requisite for the making of an order. Equally, the absence of some exceptional feature would not, it is suggested, operate as a defence.

Cases which, in the circumstances, render a non-party costs order just will fall outside of "the ordinary run of cases" (per *Dymocks*) in which

---

[41] *Dymocks Franchise Systems (NSW) Pty Ltd v Todd* [2004] 1 WLR 2807, at paragraph 25 per Lord Brown.

[42] *Travelers Insurance Company Ltd v XYZ* [2019] UKSC 48, at paragraphs 106 – 109 per Lord Reed.

the normal rules as to costs apply. In that sense, they may be described as "exceptional", but this tells us nothing about the exceptional features one should be alive to. By itself, therefore, "exceptionality" is too unspecific to be of practical assistance. It is, to quote Lord Reed in *Travelers,* "in reality little if any significance..."[43] and arguments based on the mere exceptionality of the facts alone should be treated with caution.

## 2. Pure Funders

In *Dymocks*, Lord Brown said: "Generally speaking the discretion will not be exercised against pure funders."[44]

His lordship continued to define a "pure funder" by reference to his own earlier judgment in *Hamilton v Al Fayed (No 2)* [2002] EWCA Civ 665 as: "those with no personal interest in the litigation, who do not stand to benefit from it, are not funding it as a matter of business, and in no way seek to control its course..."[45]

The *Hamilton* case arose following the high-profile lawsuit of businessman Mohamed Al-Fayed by former MP Neil Hamilton for libel. The profile of the case is relevant because it assisted the impecunious Mr Hamilton to establish what was described as a "fighting fund" to which several hundred people anonymously donated. A large portion of Mr Hamilton's legal costs were met by the fund. The donors to the fund: had no obligation to donate; exercised no control over the conduct of Mr Hamilton's case (including how their money was spent);

---

43 *Travelers Insurance Company Ltd v XYZ* [2019] UKSC 48, at paragraph 112 per Lord Reed.

44 *Dymocks Franchise Systems (NSW) Pty Ltd v Todd* [2004] 1 WLR 2807, at paragraph 25 per Lord Brown.

45 *Hamilton v Al Fayed (No 2)* [2002] EWCA Civ 665, at paragraph 40 per Simon Brown LJ.

and only expected to have their money returned if his case were successful.

Mr Hamilton's claim failed and Mr Al-Fayed, who was awarded his costs, sought an order that they be met by donors to the fighting fund.

The Court of Appeal found, albeit reluctantly, that "the unfunded party's ability to recover his costs must yield to the funded party's right of access to the courts to litigate the dispute in the first place."[46] The court reiterated what it described as "the governing principle" stated in *Abraham v Thompson* [1997] 4 All ER 362 by Millett LJ:

> *"It may be unjust to a successful defendant to be left with unrecovered costs, but the plaintiff's freedom of access to the courts has priority ... It is preferable that a successful defendant should suffer the injustice of irrecoverable costs than that a plaintiff with a genuine claim should be prevented from pursuing it."*[47]

Simon Brown LJ (as he then was) in *Hamilton* concluded:

> *"in my judgment the pure funding of litigation (whether of claims or defences) ought generally to be regarded as being in the public interest providing only and always that its essential motivation is to enable the party funded to litigate what the funders perceive to be a genuine case."*[48]

It is evident that this judgment is largly based on policy. The court noted that, had the matter been decided for Mr Al-Fayed, people may

---

[46] *Hamilton v Al Fayed (No 2)* [2002] EWCA Civ 665, at paragraph 45 per Simon Brown LJ.

[47] *Abraham v Thompson* [1997] 4 All ER 362, at 377 per Millett LJ.

[48] *Hamilton v Al Fayed (No 2)* [2002] EWCA Civ 665, at paragraph 47 per Simon Brown LJ.

be less willing to contribute to charitable funds to meet litigation costs, recognised by the court as an obvious social good. However, this view is also consistent with Phillips LJ's dictum in *Murphy v Young & Co.'s Brewery Plc.* [1997] 1 WLR 1591 that "funding alone will not justify an order against the funder under section 51."[49] The emphasis placed on the motivation[50] of the funders accords with, and foreshadows, the approach to determining "the real party" or "a real party", articulated by Lord Brown (as he later became) in *Dymocks,* discussed in Chapter 2.

The overall principle that can be derived from pure funders cases is that, whilst the funding of litigation will be a useful starting point, more will be required before the courts will consider it just to make a non-party costs order. Generally, the court will look to the motivation of the funder and their interest in the litigation. In this regard, it will be useful to compare pure funders to the position of commercial funders discussed in Chapter 6.

Since the decision in *Hamilton,* the courts have generally, though not invariably,[51] continued to be reluctant to impose third party costs orders against those family, friends and associates who, motivated by the interests of access to justice, assist a party to come to court for philanthropic and disinterested reasons. However, as is clear from the above, those reasons will require close examination in each case.

---

[49] *Murphy v Young & Co.'s Brewery Plc.* [1997] 1 WLR 1591, at 1603 per Phillips LJ.

[50] See also *Hamilton v Al Fayed (No 2)* [2002] EWCA Civ 665 at paragraph 86 per Hale LJ: "*There must, however, be exceptional cases where it would be quite unjust not to make an order: principally where the litigation was oppressive or malicious or pursued for some other ulterior motive. The fact that it was quite unmeritorious would be powerful evidence of ulterior motive but neither a necessary nor a sufficient criterion in itself.*"

[51] cf. *Kazakhstan Kagazy Plc. and others v Zhunus (formerly Zhunussov) and others* [2019] EWHC 2630 (Comm).

### 3. *Causation*

There have been shifting attitudes to the question of causation – the extent to which the costs sought from a non-party need strictly be incurred by them – in the caselaw:

In *Global Equities Ltd v Globe Legal Services Ltd* [1999] All ER (D) 226 Morritt LJ held that proof causation will be required "to some extent".[52]

However, in *Hamilton*, it was said that that "proof of causation is a necessary precondition to the making of a section 51 order against a non-party".[53]

In *Dymocks* Lord Brown said:

> *"Although the position may well be different when a number of non-parties act in concert, their Lordships are content to assume for the purposes of this application that a non-party could not ordinarily be made liable for costs if those costs would in any event have been incurred even without such non-party's involvement in the proceedings."*[54]

In *Arkin v Borchard Lines Ltd (Nos 2 and 3)* [2005] EWCA Civ 655 Lord Phillips MR said:

> *"Causation is usually a vital factor when considering whether to make an award of costs against a party. Causation is also often a*

[52] *Global Equities Ltd v Globe Legal Services Ltd* [1999] All ER (D) 226, at paragraph 28 per Morritt LJ.

[53] *Hamilton v Al Fayed (No 2)* [2002] EWCA Civ 665 at paragraph 54 per Simon Brown LJ.

[54] See also *Systemcare UK Ltd v Services Design Tech Ltd* [2011] EWCA Civ 546, at paragraph 23 per Lewison J.

> *vital factor in leading a court to make a costs order against a non-party. If the non-party is wholly or partly responsible for the fact that litigation has taken place, justice may demand that he indemnify the successful party for the costs he has incurred."*[55]

In *Total Spares & Supplies Ltd v Antares SRL* [2006] EWHC 1537 (Ch) David Richards J said:

> *"it cannot in my judgment any longer be said that causation is a necessary pre-condition to an order for costs against* [sic] *non-party. Causation will often be a vital factor but there may be cases where, in accordance with principle, it is just to make an order for costs against a non-party who cannot be said to have caused the costs in question."*[56]

In that case, however, there was still a causal link between the non-party's actions and the claimant's costs recovery in that he had deprived the claimant of any realistic opportunity of recovering its costs. The link was with the recovery of costs rather than the incurring of costs.

In *Turvill v Bird and others* [2016] EWCA Civ 703, the court declined to disturb the non-party costs order of the court below which was challenged, in part, on the grounds of causation. Hamblen LJ held, reviewing the authorities and apparently approving the wording of Morritt LJ in *Globe Equities* cited above, that causation is required "to some extent" but "is not a necessary pre-condition".[57]

---

[55] *Arkin v Borchard Lines Ltd (Nos 2 and 3)* [2005] EWCA Civ 655, at paragraphs 23 – 24 per Lord Phillips MR.

[56] *Total Spares & Supplies Ltd v Antares SRL* [2006] EWHC 1537 (Ch), at paragraph 54 per David Richards J.

[57] *Turvill v Bird and others* [2016] EWCA Civ 703, at paragraph 28 per Hamblen LJ.

Recently, in *Travelers*, the Supreme Court was eager to emphasise the importance of causation in the non-party costs jurisdiction:

> *"causation remains an important element in what an applicant under section 51 has to prove, namely a causative link between the particular conduct of the non-party relied upon and the incurring by the claimant of the costs sought to be recovered under section 51. If all those costs would have been incurred in any event, it is unlikely that a section 51 order ought to be made".*[58]

Causation is clearly therefore an important component in assessing the merits of an application for a non-party costs order. Given its judicial treatment and the broad ambit of the court's discretion, causation is unlikely to strictly be a "pre-condition", as stated in *Hamilton*. Nevertheless, causation of the costs sought "to some extent" will no doubt remain a persuasive and an important element of what an applicant for a non-party costs order must prove.

It may be that the discussion of causation is somewhat academic with respect to "the real party" principle, since it is difficult to imagine a situation in which a non-party found to be "the real party" could not be said to have caused an opponent to incur litigation costs. Consideration of causation may therefore be more relevant when a non-party is said to be "a real party" or an intermeddler.

### 4. *Impropriety*

A non-party's impropriety may be a highly relevant factor in the exercise of the court's discretion; however, its absence will not prevent the court making a costs order against them.

---

[58] *Travelers Insurance Company Ltd v XYZ* [2019] UKSC 48, at paragraph 80 per Lord Briggs.

As has been seen, the court is often concerned with the reason why a non-party has become involved in proceedings. For example, an improper motive in what would otherwise be a pure funder case[59] or in the context of company directors (see Chapter 7), can be determinative. However, though an improper motivation may be one factor in support of a non-party costs order, it is not a pre-requisite to the exercise of the discretion, as confirmed by Lord Brown in *Dymocks*:

> *"The authorities establish that, whilst any impropriety or the pursuit of speculative litigation may of itself support the making of an order against a non-party, its absence does not preclude the making of such an order."*[60]

Additionally, apart from more abstract considerations of improper motivation, improper conduct by the non-party *during* the proceedings may be of relevance. This is reflected in the concept of unjustified intermeddling (see Chapters 2 and 4) and in relation to witnesses (Chapter 5) and solicitors (Chapter 9). In *Flatman v Germany (Law Society intervening); Weddall v Barchester Health Care Ltd (Same intervening)* [2013] 1 WLR 2676, Leveson LJ confirmed:

> *"The conduct of the non-party in the course of the litigation and other than as a pure witness of material fact is of relevance and potential weight."*[61]

---

[59] See *Hamilton v Al Fayed (No 2)* [2002] EWCA Civ 665, at paragraph 86 per Hale LJ, cited above.

[60] *Dymocks Franchise Systems (NSW) Pty Ltd v Todd and others* [2004] 1 WLR 2807, at paragraph 33 per Lord Brown. That the pursuit of speculative litigation is in the same category and to be viewed in the same way as impropriety for these purposes was noted in *Goodwood Recoveries Ltd v Breen* [2005] EWCA Civ 414, at paragraphs 58 – 59 per Rix LJ.

[61] *Flatman v Germany (Law Society intervening); Weddall v Barchester Health Care Ltd (Same intervening)* [2013] 1 WLR 2676, at 2691 per Leveson LJ.

As will be seen, the parties can be bound by the court's findings of facts in the main action, including any finding of impropriety. Impropriety can therefore be an important, if not necessary, additional factor that might satisfy the court it would be appropriate to make a non-party costs order.

5. *A Non-Party Costs Application Should Not Be Used as a Substitute for the Pursuit of a Related Cause of Action Against the Non-Party in Ordinary Proceedings*

This principle emerges from *Symphony*, an early case in which the Court of Appeal sought to offer general guidance on the exercise of the non-party costs discretion and the procedure for hearing such applications. However, the ratio of the case, as confirmed by the Supreme Court in *Travelers*,[62] concerns this principle. It is well-illustrated by *Symphony's* facts.

*Symphony* involved the former employee of a kitchen unit manufacturer, Symphony, who left his job for a competitor, Halvanto, in breach of various restrictive covenants contained in his employment contract. Halvanto's solicitors provided the former employee with legal advice to the effect that Symphony had repudiated the contract. Symphony issued a claim against their former employee for damages and an injunction. The former employee was granted an emergency legal aid certificate and Halvanto's solicitors thereby continued to act for him under its terms.

Symphony succeeded at trial and, being unable to recover costs from the former employee, sought and obtained a non-party costs order against Halvanto at first instance. That order was quashed by the Court of Appeal, which held that:

---

[62] *Travelers Insurance Company Ltd v XYZ* [2019] UKSC 48, at paragraph 29 per Lord Briggs.

> *"It is clear that Symphony has at all material times had a cause of action in tort against Halvanto… [Sympony's application relies on] issues which could have been raised by Symphony against Halvanto if Halvanto had been joined as a party to the action. …it would be unjust to Halvanto to allow these issues to be raised now in this summary procedure where Halvanto has been deprived of any legal right to control the action… and of all the procedural protection to which it would have been entitled if the claim had been brought against it by action in the normal and proper way."*[63]

This principle finds expression in the reasoning of the Court of Appeal in *Deutsche Bank A.G. v Sebastian Holdings Inc. and Alexander Vik* [2016] EWCA Civ 23, which summarised:

*"When an order for costs is sought against a third party, the critical factor in each case is the nature and degree of his connection with the proceedings, since that will ultimately determine whether it is appropriate to adopt a summary procedure of the kind envisaged in the authorities…"*[64]

A party will therefore not be subject to a non-party costs order unless it can be said that the summary procedure adopted is fair. The summary procedure should not concern issues that could – but did not – form a further cause of action to which the non-party could have been joined.

6. <u>*Security for Costs*</u>

Rule 25.13 of the Civil Procedure Rules 1998 ('CPR') provides, in part:

[63] *Symphony Group Plc. v Hodgson* [1994] QB 179, at 194 – 195 per Balcombe LJ.

[64] *Deutsche Bank A.G. v Sebastian Holdings Inc. and Alexander Vik* [2016] EWCA Civ 23, at paragraph 21 per Moore-Bick LJ.

*25.13*

*(1) The court may make an order for security for costs under rule 25.12 if–*

*(a) it is satisfied, having regard to all the circumstances of the case, that it is just to make such an order; and*

*(b)*

*(i) one or more of the conditions in paragraph (2) applies, or*

*(ii) an enactment permits the court to require security for costs*

*(2) The conditions are –*

*...*

*(f) the claimant is acting as a nominal claimant, other than as a representative claimant under Part 19, and there is reason to believe that he will be unable to pay the defendant's costs if ordered to do so;*

Applications for non-party costs orders are often motivated by the impecuniosity of the losing party to the litigation. It is sometimes argued by a non-party that a successful defendant should have applied for security for costs from the claimant and their failure to do so renders it unjust to make a non-party costs order against them.

Though similarities between CPR 25.13(2)(f) and the non-party costs jurisdiction have been recognised,[65] the Court of Appeal has confirmed that "...a failure to apply for security does not preclude a successful application for an order for costs against a third party."[66]

[65] See *Dymocks Franchise Systems (NSW) Pty Ltd v Todd and others* [2004] 1 WLR 2807, at paragraph 25 per Lord Brown.

[66] *Deutsche Bank A.G. v Sebastian Holdings Inc. and Alexander Vik* [2016] EWCA Civ 23, at paragraphs 48 – 51 per Moore-Bick LJ.

Equally, it has been argued that a successful application for security for costs inhibits the engagement of the non-party costs jurisdiction altogether. That argument was discussed in *Petromec Inc. v Petroleo Brasileiro SA Petrobras* [2006] EWCA Civ 1038 in which the court said:

> *"This puts the matter much too high. The ability to obtain an order for security for costs and the existence of any security put up as a result of such order are matters which a judge has to take into consideration… But the fact that in the course of the proceedings a judge (Andrew Smith J in this case) ordered security which, in the event, has turned out to be inadequate should not be any reason for declining to exercise jurisdiction in an otherwise appropriate case. As the [trial] judge said in paragraph 43 'it is no more unjust to make the backers of an insolvent company liable for the costs… than it is to require them to provide security for costs on its behalf.'"*[67]

Accordingly, whilst the existence or otherwise of security may be a factor in an appropriate case the two jurisdictions remain distinct. It is certainly not the case that the engagement of one jurisdiction (or lack thereof) determines the course of the other.

*7. Warning*

It is wise for applicants for non-party costs orders to warn the intended non-party of their intention as soon as possible. However, the effect such a warning will have on the exercise of the discretion depends on the circumstances of the case. Balcombe LJ said in *Symphony* that the applicant:

[67] *Petromec Inc. v Petroleo Brasileiro SA Petrobras* [2006] EWCA Civ 1038, at paragraph 14 per Longmore LJ.

> *"should warn the non-party at the earliest opportunity of the possibility that he may seek to apply for costs against him... [this is] an obvious application of the basic principles of natural justice."*[68]

Nevertheless, it is clear from the subsequent decisions that have interpreted the relatively early case of *Symphony* that a warning is not a prerequisite to a successful application. To treat it as such was said by the court in *Deutsche Bank* "to read too much into the Symphony guidelines".[69] The usual approach is for the court to consider what, if any, difference a warning would have made to the progress of the litigation and thereby the incurrence of costs. In *Dymocks*, Lord Brown said, citing Australian authority:

> *"Mr Dale relies upon Dymocks' failure to warn Associated of their intention to make this application until after the Board's decision on the substantive appeal. The authorities establish, however, that this is no more than a material consideration in the case (see, for example, Knight v FP Special Assets Ltd and Kebaro Pty Ltd v Saunders [2003] FCAFC 5) and their Lordships are unable to see how an earlier warning could have made any difference to the course of the proceedings here."*[70]

In *Deutsche Bank*, the Court of Appeal rejected, in passing, the argument that an applicant is under an obligation to explain why a warning was not given. Moore-Bick LJ confirmed that "The importance of a

---

[68] *Symphony Group Plc. v Hodgson* [1994] QB 179, at 193 per Balcombe LJ.

[69] *Deutsche Bank A.G. v Sebastian Holdings Inc. and Alexander Vik* [2016] EWCA Civ 23, at paragraph 32 per Moore-Bick LJ.

[70] *Dymocks Franchise Systems (NSW) Pty Ltd v Todd and others* [2004] 1 WLR 2807, at paragraph 31 per Lord Brown.

warning will vary from case to case and may depend on the extent to which it would have affected the course of the proceedings…"[71]

An illustration of that reasoning is found in *Kazakhstan Kagazy Plc. and others v Zhunus (formerly Zhunussov) and others* [2019] EWHC 2630 (Comm), a pure funder case involving a wife's support of her husband's litigation. Jacobs J, granting the application in that case explained:

> *"Furthermore, even if a warning had been given, I regard it as wholly improbable that [the non-party funders] Mrs. Arip, or indeed Ms. Asilbekova, would have acted differently. It is in my view fanciful to think that a warning would have led either of them to decide that they were no longer prepared to support [the Second Defendant] Mr. Arip's defence. Indeed, Mrs. Arip's evidence was that it was inconceivable that a wife would fail to support their husband in circumstances where he would have lost the ability to defend himself. In fact, Mrs. Arip continued to fund Mr. Arip's costs after the judge had rejected his case and held him to have acted dishonestly throughout."*[72]

An example of where a warning was relevant is found in *Sony/ATV Music Publishing LLC and another company v WPMC Ltd (in liquidation) and others* [2018] EWCA Civ 2005, which concerned the director of the defendant company. The director's evidence was summarised by Floyd LJ:

> *"As to the absence of warning, [the non-party director] Mr Bailey had said in his evidence that if he had been warned prior to trial*

[71] *Deutsche Bank A.G. v Sebastian Holdings Inc. and Alexander Vik* [2016] EWCA Civ 23, at paragraph 32 per Moore-Bick LJ.

[72] *Kazakhstan Kagazy Plc. and others v Zhunus (formerly Zhunussov) and others* [2019] EWHC 2630 (Comm), at paragraph 101 per Jacobs J.

> *that he might face a [non-party costs order] NPCO he would either have put [the Defendant company] WPMC into liquidation or accepted one of [the Claimant's] SATV's settlement offers. Further he said that if he had been warned after the trial he would have tried to raise funds to enable the appeal for which permission had been granted to be pursued… By 7 July 2016, when the warning was given, WPMC was long out of time for filing an appellant's notice."*[73]

After discussing the various other grounds of appeal, his lordship concluded:

> *"Thus far I would regard matters as fairly evenly balanced. It might be said that Mr Bailey, standing as he did to benefit from the outcome, was 'a real party' if not the only one. However, the absence of any form of warning is, in my judgment, fatal to the application for the NPCO."*[74]

Therefore, it seems that determining the importance of a warning in a particular case is a fact-specific enquiry as to what, if any, difference such a warning would have made to the course of the litigation. To that end, it is noteworthy that, in *Deutsche Bank*, Moore-Bick LJ made the logical observation that:

> *"If the third party against whom an order for costs is sought is <u>the</u> real party to the litigation, the absence of a warning may be of little consequence."*[75] *[emphasis added]*

---

[73] *Sony/ATV Music Publishing LLC and another company v WPMC Ltd (in liquidation) and others* [2018] EWCA Civ 2005, at paragraph 43 per Floyd LJ.

[74] *Sony/ATV Music Publishing LLC and another company v WPMC Ltd (in liquidation) and others* [2018] EWCA Civ 2005, at paragraph 86 per Floyd LJ.

[75] *Deutsche Bank A.G. v Sebastian Holdings Inc. and Alexander Vik* [2016] EWCA Civ 23, at paragraph 32 per Moore-Bick LJ.

It may therefore be inferred that where a party seeks to establish a non-party's liability as "a real party" or as an intermeddler, the absence of a warning may be more relevant to the exercise of the court's jurisdiction depending on the facts of the case.

# PART TWO
# SPECIFIC NON-PARTIES

Though the courts have struggled to identify principles applicable across the board, they have been more willing to develop clearer guidance with respect to certain non-parties against whom non-party costs orders have frequently been sought. These more specific principles mostly take the general principles discussed in Part 1 as their starting point. In addition to providing discrete guidance, they indicate how courts may deal with novel situations by analogy. This part will summarise and discuss the principles in relation to seven categories of non-party.

# CHAPTER FOUR
# LIABILITY INSURERS

## *The Role of Insurers*

Liability insurers – that is to say those who indemnify their insured in respect of sums arising out of litigation – are common targets for non-party costs applications.

The function of liability insurers, in the normal run of cases, is both to meet their insured's own legal expenses and indemnify their insured against liability they incur in litigation. This liability can include meeting an adverse costs order.

In the event the insured is or becomes insolvent, the beneficiary of an order is assisted by the Third Parties (Rights Against Insurers) Act 2010. This makes it easier for them to make a claim directly against an insurer and thereby avoid the more protracted and indirect route of enforcing an order against the insolvent subject of an order.

In the event that any part of an award against the insured falls outside the terms of the insurance policy, it is expected to be met by the insured personally. The indemnity an insurer provides is, after all, merely a contractual obligation between them and their insured; the arrangement should not, at first blush, concern the beneficiary of the order at all – even where the insured is unable to pay.

Given the obvious interest insurers have in the outcome of proceedings for which they provide cover, they will almost inevitably have the right to exercise a degree of control over the conduct of the proceedings, notwithstanding the fact that – ordinarily – they are not, themselves, a party. The position was explained by Sir Wilfred Greene MR in *Groom v Crocker* [1939] 1 KB 194:

> *"The right given to the insurers is to have control of proceedings in which they and the assured have a common interest – the assured because he is the defendant and the insurers because they are contractually bound to indemnify him. Each is interested in seeing that any judgment to be recovered against the assured shall be for as small a sum as possible."*[76]

Although the control a non-party has over proceedings is an important factor to consider (see Chapter 2), it cannot – for this reason alone – be said that an insurer exercising control over the case they fund makes it "the real party" or "a real party". Neither (per *Groom*, above) can it be said that such an insurer is unjustifiably intermeddling in the case.

The caselaw discussing the non-party costs liability of insurers discloses two broad types of case which merit discussion.

The first is where the claim falls within the scope of insurance but where the burden of an order for costs (on top of any order for damages) exceeds the policy cover limit.

The second is where the claim or part of a claim does not fall within the scope of insurance, but the insurer nonetheless involves itself in the conduct of litigation.

In the former case, the principle of the insurer's involvement is established. The relevant question is whether the insurer has acted as "the real party" or "a real party" such that the court is – for that reason – justified in imposing a liability that the contract did not contemplate. In the latter case, the principle of the insurer's involvement is not as clear. The relevant questions in establishing whether the insurer is "unjustifiably intermeddling" in the litigation are the extent of, and justification for, its involvement.

---

[76] *Groom v Crocker* [1939] 1 KB 194, at 203 per Sir Wilfred Greene MR.

*Limits of Cover Cases*

The starting point is the case of *T.G.A. Chapman Ltd v Christopher* [1998] 1 WLR 12 in which the insured defendant (who was personally insolvent) was successfully sued in negligence, his defence failing in its entirety. He was held liable for £1.2m in damages and ordered to pay the claimant's costs. The defendant was insured for losses he negligently incurred but his insurers' liability was limited to £1m – a sum insufficient to cover all the damages awarded, let alone the costs. Though the policy indemnified the defendant, by virtue of the Third Parties (Rights against Insurers) Act 1930[77] the defendant's insurers were also contingently liable to the Claimant.

Crucially, as the defendant was insolvent throughout and would have been content to settle the case at the outset, the insurer made the decision to contest the litigation. It also financed and conducted the defence, evidently in an attempt to avoid or reduce its own liability.

A non-party costs order was made against the defendant's insurers. On appeal, affirming the non-party costs order, Phillips LJ noted that the insurers: determined that the claim would be fought; funded the defence of the claim; had the conduct of the litigation and, crucially, fought the claim exclusively to defend their own interests. His lordship held that, in a "paradigm case" of this kind, the insurers "were the defendants in all but name."[78]

The most important element of this finding was that the insurers were motivated by defending solely their own interests, as opposed to those of the insured. The insurer's control and funding of the matter follow from the policy of insurance. However, where the insured has no

[77] The predecessor to the Third Parties (Rights against Insurers) Act 2010.

[78] *T.G.A. Chapman Ltd v Christopher* [1998] 1 WLR 12, at paragraph 22 per Phillips LJ.

interest in defending the claim, and the insurers continue, they adopt a renewed responsibility for the consequences. Phillips LJ explained:

> *"To make such an order is not to rewrite the policy. It is to impose on underwriters a liability which is independent of the policy."*[79]

Importantly, it was not suggested that the insurers had exceeded the bounds of their rights and obligations under the policy. Phillips LJ confirmed that is not determinative with respect to applying the "the real party" principle in this context.

Following *Chapman*, the courts have emphasised the importance of three factors Phillips LJ mentioned in dealing with limits of cover cases.[80] These are that the insurer:

1. determined that the claim would be fought;

2. had the conduct of the litigation; and

3. fought the claim exclusively to defend their own interests.

These have become known as "the Chapman principles". Though not rigid rules, they are guidelines for the court to follow in such cases.

As to the first two principles, we have seen that, given their obvious financial interest in their insured's case, insurers often have considerable (if not determinative) influence over whether claims will be fought or settled (per *Groom*, above). It is not uncommon for the insurer to

---

[79] *T.G.A. Chapman Ltd v Christopher* [1998] 1 WLR 12, at paragraph 22 per Phillips LJ.

[80] See *Citibank NA v Excess Insurance Co Ltd* [1999] Lloyd's Rep IR 122; and *Travelers Insurance Company Ltd v XYZ* [2019] UKSC 48, at paragraphs 37 – 41 per Lord Briggs.

have conduct of the litigation as a form of compulsory agency over the insured.

The third principle is therefore crucial in determining liability. In *Cormack v Washbourne* [2000] Lloyd's Rep PN 459 the Court of Appeal held that – in a limit of cover case – a "critical ingredient" was the extent to which "the insurer's conduct of the action was sufficiently self-motivated to the exclusion of the defendant's interest".[81] Of course, it is inevitable that insurers will be self-motivated to defend a claim brought against their insured. But in *Cormack*, the court held that it will be necessary to consider whether the insurers have strayed beyond an appropriate balance and allowed their own interests to *predominate* over those of the insured, as they evidently did in *Chapman*.[82]

That is not to say the enquiry is solely about the insured's motivation to defend the claim or the fact that an insurer has a *greater* interest in defending the claim. Rather, it is important to ask whether it can be said that the insurer is acting predominately in their own interests such as to make it just to treat them as "the real party" they effectively become.

This approach underscores the potential importance of causation (see Chapter 3) as a general principle. An insurer who defends a claim in the name of an insured who has no interest themselves in doing so can be said to have caused the party to incur the liability of any costs order that is made. In circumstances where the party had no interest in pursuing the matter and adopting the attendant risk in causing costs to be incurred, it will seldom be just to make him liable for them. The importance of an enquiry into the causation of the costs in the

[81] *Cormack v Washbourne* [2000] Lloyd's Rep PN 459, at paragraph 35 per Auld LJ.

[82] See *Cormack v Washbourne* [2000] Lloyd's Rep PN 459, at paragraph 35 per Auld LJ.

insurance context was recently affirmed by the Supreme Court in *Travelers Insurance Co Ltd v XYZ* [2019] UKSC 48.[83]

<u>*Lack of Coverage Cases*</u>

Where the question is not about the contractual limitations of cover, but as to the existence of cover at all, it will generally be necessary to apply the intermeddling principle.[84]

The Supreme Court in *Travelers* recently gave guidance about the application of this principle in the insurance context. Giving the lead judgment, Lord Briggs explained that:

> *"Its starting assumption is that non-parties usually, although not invariably, have no legitimate interest in becoming involved in the litigation of others. It does not render involvement of any kind objectionable, but only involvement which is (in old-fashioned language) wanton and officious, for which the non-party cannot demonstrate some justification or excuse."*[85]

It follows that, in the insurance context, the starting point in evaluating liability as an intermeddler will generally be an examination of the policy of insurance since this is ordinarily what justifies an insurer's involvement. According to Lord Briggs in *Travelers*, whether the non-party has "become involved under a framework of contractual obligation is likely to be of primary relevance. It may even be decisive against

[83] See *Travelers Insurance Company Ltd v XYZ* [2019] UKSC 48, at paragraphs 65 – 67 per Lord Briggs.

[84] See *Travelers Insurance Company Ltd v XYZ* [2019] UKSC 48.

[85] *Travelers Insurance Company Ltd v XYZ* [2019] UKSC 48, at paragraph 54 per Lord Briggs.

liability."[86] Contractual entitlement, though likely to be of central importance in the insurance context, is not the only way the non-party can justify its involvement, however; it must simply be able to evidence *some* interest in the litigation recognised by law.[87]

Sometimes, for example, an insurer becomes involved in a matter comprising both insured and uninsured claims, as the facts of *Travelers* illustrate.

*Travelers* involved a large-scale group action claim against Transform, a medical group who were covered by insurance only up to a certain point during their trading life. 623 claimants sued Transform for the supply of defective silicone implants. Transform was insured in respect of 197 claims, which were ultimately settled. The remaining 426 claims were successful, however Transform entered insolvent administration during the litigation, leaving those claimants unable to recover any damages or their costs. They applied to for a non-party costs order against the insurer who was involved in the defence of the suit throughout.

Here, where an insurer becomes involved in cases for which they do not provide cover as an almost-inevitable consequence of defending those for which they do, the Supreme Court held that they will not be liable for a non-party costs order as an intermeddler because their involvement in defending the entirety of the claim was justified:

> *"there [was] a connection between uninsured claims and claims for which the insurer had provided cover, it may well be that the legitimate interests of the insurer would justify some involvement by the*

---

[86] *Travelers Insurance Company Ltd v XYZ* [2019] UKSC 48, at paragraph 55 per Lord Briggs.

[87] See *Travelers Insurance Company Ltd v XYZ* [2019] UKSC 48, at paragraph 116 per Lord Sumption.

> *insurer in decision-making and even funding of the defence of the uninsured claims without exposing the insurer to liability to pay the successful claimant's costs.*"[88]

Giving the main judgment, Lord Briggs evaluated those aspects of the insurer's conduct which were said to qualify as intermeddling against the justification for that conduct. This included the insurer not disclosing the limits of cover and not authorising offers or admissions in respect of the uninsured claimants.[89] Overall, the court concluded that the insurer's conduct did not cross the line to become unjustified intermeddling.

Finally, even where established, it seems that unjustified intermeddling by itself will not be sufficient to establish liability unless it can be said to have some causal link to the costs sought.[90] The court has a wide discretion as to the form of the non-party costs order (see Chapter 11) and may therefore restrict the quantum of an order to the sum attributable to that portion of the intermeddling for which there is no justification.

---

[88] *Travelers Insurance Company Ltd v XYZ* [2019] UKSC 48, at paragraph 79 per Lord Briggs.

[89] See *Travelers Insurance Company Ltd v XYZ* [2019] UKSC 48, at paragraphs 63 – 64 and 70 – 71 per Lord Briggs.

[90] See *Travelers Insurance Company Ltd v XYZ* [2019] UKSC 48, at paragraphs 65 – 67 and 73 – 74 per Lord Briggs; and *Cormack v Washbourne* [2000] Lloyd's Rep PN 459.

# CHAPTER FIVE
# WITNESSES

It is rare that witnesses are made subject to a non-party costs order. There may be something of a tension between this jurisdiction and the principle of witness immunity, as articulated by Lord Hutton in *Darker v Chief Constable of the West* Midlands [2001] 1 AC 435:

> *"The rule that a party has immunity in respect of what he says and does in court has been established for centuries."*[91]

However, in *Symphony Group Plc. v Hodgson* [1994] QB 179, Balcombe LJ suggested that the court was not restricted in its ability to make a non-party costs order against a witness:

> *"(7) Again, the normal rule is that witnesses in either civil or criminal proceedings enjoy immunity from any form of civil action in respect of evidence given during those proceedings. ... In so far as the evidence of a witness in proceedings may lead to an application for the costs of those proceedings against him or his company, it introduces yet another exception to a valuable general principle."*[92]

In *Deutsche Bank A.G. v Sebastian Holdings Inc. and Alexander Vik* [2016] EWCA Civ 23, Moore-Bick LJ said, in reference to the passage of Balcombe LJ cited above:

> *"In Symphony v Hodgson the court in its seventh guideline appears to have recognised that there may be cases in which it will be just to make an order for costs (not necessarily the whole costs of the action)*

[91] *Darker v Chief Constable of the West* Midlands [2001] 1 AC 435, at 465 per Lord Hutton.

[92] *Symphony Group Plc. v Hodgson* [1994] QB 179, at 193 per Balcombe LJ.

> *against a witness and we do not think that the possibility should be excluded. The power to make such an order should, however, be exercised with considerable care. To make an order for costs against a witness simply because he has given false evidence might well infringe the principles of witness immunity, but to make such an order on the grounds that he had conspired with others to pursue a claim that was entirely fabricated would not, even if in order to support it he had given false evidence.*"[93]

It was acknowledged in *Darker*, however, that witness immunity did not extend to the fabrication of evidence.[94] Therefore it is perhaps doubtful in light of *Deutsche Bank* that the non-party costs jurisdiction can really be said to be an "exception", as suggested in *Symphony.*

In cases concerning the potential costs liability of non-party witnesses – as a result of their testimony alone[95] – it is suggested that it may be more appropriate to apply the intermeddling principle and consider what additional costs may have been incurred as a result of, for example, fabricated evidence. This is a situation where one might expect to see the expansion of that principle outside of the insurance context, but it has yet to be fully considered by the courts. At present, however, it seems clear that the application of the non-party costs jurisdiction with respect to witnesses is narrow.

---

[93] *Deutsche Bank A.G. v Sebastian Holdings Inc. and Alexander Vik* [2016] EWCA Civ 23, at paragraph 44 per Moore-Bick LJ.

[94] *Darker v Chief Constable of the West* Midlands [2001] 1 AC 435, at 471 – 472 per Lord Hutton; See also *Autofocus Ltd v Accident Exchange Ltd* [2010] EWCA Civ 788.

[95] Unlike the facts of Deutsche Bank, where the non-party witness not only fabricated evidence but also was a director of the defendant company and clearly "the real party".

# CHAPTER SIX
# COMMERCIAL LITIGATION FUNDERS

The prevalence of commercial litigation funding and the "endless development of novel ways of funding the ever-increasing cost of litigation"[96] has provoked the development of specific principles applicable to defining commercial funders' costs liability as a non-party.

Commercial litigation funders generally rank among the most vulnerable to non-party costs orders. However, as will be seen, each case – and each funding arrangement – will have to be closely examined by the court.

## *The Principle of Liability*

In *Hamilton v Al Fayed (No 2)* [2002] EWCA Civ 665, the Court of Appeal dismissed an application for a non-party costs order against "pure funders" (see Chapter 3). The court held that the pure funding of litigation was in the public interest provided that its essential motivation was to enable the funded party to litigate what the funders perceived to be a genuine case. Importantly, though they enabled the claim to be bought, the pure funders were obviously not "real parties" to the litigation (see Chapter 2) and stood to gain nothing[97] from the litigation's success.

In contrast, a commercial funder is an investor who hopes to make a return on his investment. A typical commercial funding contract will

[96] *Travelers Insurance Company Ltd v XYZ* [2019] UKSC 48, at paragraph 27 per Lord Briggs.

[97] Other than to be reimbursed their contribution.

provide for all or part of a party's legal costs to be met by the funder in exchange for a share of the proceeds if the party is successful. If the case is lost, the funder bears their costs and there is nothing to be repaid. Evidently, the essential motivation for funding is profit. Recalling that the "only immutable principle is that the discretion has to be exercised justly",[98] the courts have been willing to make non-party costs orders against commercial litigation funders as "justice will usually require that, if the funded proceedings fail, the funder or funders must pay the successful party's costs."[99]

It might be difficult to think of a commercial funder as "the real party" when they become involved only at the behest of a party (who presumably is seeking their own benefit) and may not necessarily exercise any degree of control over proceedings. Nevertheless, the fact they stand to benefit from funding the litigation will generally make them "a real party in very important and critical respects" *[emphasis added]*.[100] Commercial funders are, using the language of Lord Brown in *Dymocks Franchise Systems (NSW) Pty Ltd v Todd* [2004] 1 WLR 2807, a non-party who "not merely funds but also substantially controls or at any rate is to benefit from" proceedings and whilst "facilitating access to justice by the party funded" is also, crucially, "gaining access to justice for his own purposes."[101]

---

[98] *Deutsche Bank A.G. v Sebastian Holdings Inc. and Alexander Vik* [2016] EWCA Civ 23, at paragraph 62 per Moore-Bick LJ.

[99] *Excalibur Ventures LLC v Texas Keystone Inc. and others* [2016] EWCA Civ 1144, at paragraph 1 per Tomlinson LJ. Note also the obvious parallels with maintenance and champerty – see *Hill v Archbold* [1968] 1 QB 686, at 695 per Lord Denning: *"This is perfectly justifiable and is accepted by everyone as lawful, provided always that the one who supports the litigation, if it fails, pays the costs of the other side."*

[100] *Dymocks Franchise Systems (NSW) Pty Ltd v Todd and others* [2004] 1 WLR 2807, at paragraph 25 per Lord Brown.

[101] *Dymocks Franchise Systems (NSW) Pty Ltd v Todd and others* [2004] 1 WLR 2807, at paragraph 25 per Lord Brown.

Therefore, once commercial funders have been identified as such (i.e. motivated by the profit incentive), they usually risk some form of non-party costs liability should the funded case fail. As was said in *Hamilton v Al Fayed (No 2)* [2003] QB 1175:

> *"It would be very exceptional that a situation would arise where it would not be just and reasonable to make a s 51 order against a professional funder."*[102]

Arguments that the principle of liability is not established will typically focus on the degree of benefit (or lack thereof) to the funders of the funding bargain struck.[103] However, it was said in *Excalibur Ventures LLC v Texas Keystone Inc. and others* [2016] EWCA Civ 1144 that once a party is identified as a commercial litigation funder, realistically "no further evidential enquiry will be necessary and that the ground is adequately laid for an order under section 51(3)".[104]

Additionally, once the principle of liability has been established, Tomlinson LJ noted in *Excalibur* that the basis of assessment for the commercial funder's costs should generally be the same as the funded party, notwithstanding the funder's conduct. His lordship emphasised that:

> *"the derivative nature of a commercial funder's involvement should ordinarily lead to his being required to contribute to the costs on the*

---

102 *Hamilton v Al Fayed (No 2)* [2002] EWCA Civ 665, at paragraph 71 per Simon Brown LJ.

103 It is not completely clear from the language of *Dymocks* whether the *benefit* that stands to be gained need be "substantial". *Excalibur Ventures LLC v Texas Keystone Inc. and others* [2016] EWCA Civ 1144, at paragraph 18 per Tomlinson LJ appears to suggest so.

104 *Excalibur Ventures LLC v Texas Keystone Inc. and others* [2016] EWCA Civ 1144, at paragraph 18 per Tomlinson LJ.

> *basis upon which they have been assessed against those whom he chose to fund."*[105] *[emphasis in original]*

The claims in *Excalibur* failed on every point. The trial judge ordered the claimant to pay the defendants' costs assessed on the indemnity basis, noting:

> *"The litigation has been gargantuan in scope, involving a five-month trial and 373 trial bundles. But it was based on no sound foundation in fact or law and it has met with a resounding, indeed catastrophic, defeat."*[106]

In affirming the non-party costs order therefore, the Court of Appeal ordered the claimant's funders to meet the defendants' costs on the same basis.

<u>*The Extent of Liability*</u>

Given that commercial funders will often only pay a portion of the overall cost of litigation, the question arises as to the amount of the costs that should be paid by them if a non-party costs order is made.

The well-known case of *Arkin v Borchard Lines Ltd (Nos 2 and 3)* [2005] EWCA Civ 655 concerned a claim for substantial damages against various firms involved in international shipping on the basis that they had breached European competition rules. The claimant had no means to finance the litigation himself and therefore entered into a funding agreement with a professional funding company, MPC, who funded expert evidence in support of the claim for a contingent

---

105 *Excalibur Ventures LLC v Texas Keystone Inc. and others* [2016] EWCA Civ 1144, at paragraph 27 per Tomlinson LJ

106 *Excalibur Ventures LLC v Texas Keystone Inc. and others* [2013] EWHC 4278 (Comm), at paragraph 9 per Christopher Clarke LJ.

fee, being a percentage of any damages awarded. MPC exercised no control over the litigation. The amount of MPC's funding contribution was £1.3m.

The claimant's claim ultimately failed and, with the claimant being impecunious, the defendants applied for a non-party costs order against MPC. At first instance, the application was dismissed by the trial judge. The Court of Appeal reversed the decision of the trial judge but held that that MPC should only be liable to the extent of its contribution: £1.3m. That approach was designed to strike a balance between ensuring some, if limited, costs recovery for the successful party and not discouraging commercial funders' engagement (at a time where the commercial funding market was not as well established).[107] Consistent with the general approach of the courts to non-party costs orders explored earlier in this work, the Court of Appeal did not suggest that this was an invariable approach for courts below to adopt in all cases involving a commercial funder.[108]

Nevertheless, the decision in *Arkin* established what came to be known as the "Arkin Cap" on non-party costs liability – where a commercial funder's costs liability was limited to the extent of his financial contribution. The approach adopted in *Arkin* was followed in subsequent cases involving different types of commercial funding contracts.[109] This proved unsatisfactory in a number of respects and received criticism from the judiciary and commentators. Sir Rupert Jackson in his 2009 Review of Civil Litigation Costs said:

---

107 *Arkin v Borchard Lines Ltd (Nos 2 and 3)* [2005] EWCA Civ 655, at paragraphs 38 – 44 per Lord Phillips MR.

108 *Arkin v Borchard Lines Ltd (Nos 2 and 3)* [2005] EWCA Civ 655, at paragraph 43 per Lord Phillips MR.

109 For example, *Excalibur Ventures LLC v Texas Keystone Inc. and others* [2016] EWCA Civ 1144.

> *"In my view, it is wrong in principle that a litigation funder, which stands to recover a share of damages in the event of success, should be able to escape part of the liability for costs in the event of defeat. This is unjust not only to the opposing party (who may be left with unrecovered costs) but also to the client (who may be exposed to costs liabilities which it cannot meet).*
>
> *I recommend that either by rule change or by legislation third party funders should be exposed to liability for adverse costs in respect of litigation which they fund. The extent of the funder's liability should be a matter for the discretion of the judge in the individual case. The funder's potential liability should not be limited by the extent of its investment in the case."*[110]

The Arkin Cap came to be reconsidered recently by the Court of Appeal in *ChapelGate Credit Opportunity Master Fund Limited v Money and others* [2020] EWCA Civ 246. That case concerned a commercial funder, ChapelGate, who had supported litigation that had ultimately failed. ChapelGate accepted the principle of their costs liability but argued that it should be limited to the extent of their funding, which would have left the defendants to the main action to pay the vast majority of their costs themselves.

At first instance, Snowden J declined to follow the Court of Appeal's approach in *Arkin*:

> *"In short, what has become known as the Arkin cap is, in my judgment, best understood as an approach which the Court of Appeal in Arkin intended should be considered for application in cases involving a commercial funder as a means of achieving a just result in all the circumstances of the particular case. But I do not think that*

[110] Sir Rupert Jackson, *Review of Civil Litigation Costs: Final Report* (TSO, 2010), page 123; see also *Excalibur Ventures LLC v Texas Keystone Inc. and others* [2016] EWCA Civ 1144, at paragraph 28 per Tomlinson LJ.

> *it is a rule to be applied automatically in all cases involving commercial funders, whatever the facts, and however unjust the result of doing so might be."*[111]

On ChapelGate's appeal, the Court of Appeal confirmed that *Arkin* imposed no fetter on the discretion of the courts and, in that respect, noted that the court was not limited in the factors it could consider when applying its discretion. The *Arkin* approach focuses exclusively on one factor: the extent of the funding provided. The court held that, whilst this will be a factor to consider, other factors may also be relevant, such as – consistently with Lord Brown's dictum in *Dymocks* – the amount the funder stood to gain.[112] Newey LJ affirmed:

> *"Judges, as it seems to me, retain a discretion and, depending on the facts, may consider it appropriate to take into account matters other than the extent of the funder's funding and not to limit the funder's liability to the amount of that funding."*[113]

The "solution" arrived at in *Arkin* has not become redundant, however it should be seen as merely one option available to the courts in exercising their wide discretion on non-party costs. The Court of Appeal said that that solution is "particularly likely to be relevant on facts closely comparable to those in Arkin, where the funder had 'merely covered the costs incurred by the claimant in instructing expert

[111] *Davey v Money and another; Dunbar Assets Plc. v Davey* [2019] EWHC 997 (Ch), at paragraph 89 per Snowden J.

[112] See *ChapelGate Credit Opportunity Master Fund Limited v Money and others* [2020] EWCA Civ 246, paragraphs 35 and 38 per Newey LJ. Note that this correlates with the importance accorded to a non-party's standing to benefit in *Dymocks* and discussed elsewhere in this work (see, for example, Chapter 7).

[113] *ChapelGate Credit Opportunity Master Fund Limited v Money and others* [2020] EWCA Civ 246, paragraph 38 per Newey LJ.

witnesses'..."[114] That is to say where a discrete portion of the costs incurred can be said to have arisen from the funding provided.[115] Likewise, however, the court said:

> *"In the case of a funder who had funded the lion's share of a claimant's costs in return for the lion's share of the potential fruits of litigation against multiple parties, it would not be surprising if the judge ordered the funder to bear at least the lion's share of the winners' costs, regardless of whether the funder's outlay on the claimant's costs had been a lesser figure."*[116] *[emphasis added]*

*Arkin* can therefore no longer be said to impose a "cap", if it ever did. It is best thought of as an illustration of one possible solution when considering costs orders against non-party commercial funders. The decision in *ChapelGate* affirmed the applicability of the familiar general principle that each case, including the quantum of each order, will depend on its particular facts.

[114] *ChapelGate Credit Opportunity Master Fund Limited v Money and others* [2020] EWCA Civ 246, paragraph 37 per Newey LJ.

[115] This is consistent with the importance generally accorded to causation (see Chapter 3).

[116] *ChapelGate Credit Opportunity Master Fund Limited v Money and others* [2020] EWCA Civ 246, paragraph 38 per Newey LJ.

# CHAPTER SEVEN
# COMPANIES

Where companies bring or defend proceedings, there will almost inevitably be some degree of non-party involvement, typically from directors. In these cases, the court is usually concerned with identifying "the real party" to the litigation by looking to the motivation behind the proceedings.

In this regard, it is clear that in the normal run of cases, a director of a company who causes a company to bring or defend an action will not be made liable for costs without more. There are sound policy reasons for this, and it follows from the basic tenets of English company law. Millett LJ in *Metalloy Supplies Ltd v MA (UK) Ltd* [1997] 1 WLR 1613 said:

> *"Where such proceedings are brought bona fide and for the benefit of the company, the company is the real plaintiff. If in such a case an order for costs could be made against a director in the absence of some impropriety or bad faith on his part, the doctrine of the separate liability of the company would be eroded and the principle that such orders should be exceptional would be nullified."*[117]

The courts have been concerned with protecting company directors who do not overstep their position. As funding and/or control of the company may well be within those bounds, something more is needed to make them "the real party". As stated above, Millett LJ suggested that this would include a director's impropriety or bad faith; it is clear from subsequent caselaw however that the additional factor may also include the situation where a director brings proceedings solely for his

[117] *Metalloy Supplies Ltd v MA (UK) Ltd* [1997] 1 WLR 1613, at 1620 per Millett LJ.

own benefit. Rix LJ in *Goodwood Recoveries Ltd v Breen* [2005] EWCA Civ 414 explained that:

> *"Where a non-party director can be described as the 'real party', seeking his own benefit, controlling and/or funding the litigation, then even where he has acted in good faith or without any impropriety, justice may well demand that he be liable in costs on a fact-sensitive and objective assessment of the circumstances."*[118]

Commenting on that extract in *Systemcare UK Ltd v Services Design Tech Ltd* [2011] EWCA Civ 546, Lewison J said:

> *"It is to be noted that controlling on the one hand and funding on the other are separated by 'and/or'. Thus, it is not the case that both elements need to be present."*[119]

Again, the mere fact that a director controls or funds proceedings is not, of itself, sufficient to ground a non-party costs order. The court must also look to the interest the director has and weigh these factors that may indicate that a director is, in fact, "the real party" behind the company.

Of course, acting in litigation may be both in the interests of the company and the director, particularly if they are also a shareholder – both may well stand to gain. In this situation, it is suggested that there may be a useful analogy with limits of cover insurance cases (see Chapter 4) where it will be relevant to ask whether the director has allowed his own interests to predominate over those of the company. As was said in *Housemaker Services Ltd v Cole* [2017] EWHC 924 (Ch):

---

[118] *Goodwood Recoveries Ltd v Breen* [2005] EWCA Civ 414, at paragraph 59 per Rix LJ.

[119] *Systemcare UK Ltd v Services Design Tech Ltd* [2011] EWCA Civ 546, at paragraph 33 per Lewison J.

*"Moreover, it is not an unusual thing, let alone wrong, that a director who is a shareholder of a company and who funds the company's claim will ultimately benefit from it if it is successful. It is simply a consequence of the policies adopted by our company law, allowing businessmen to take some risks in seeking profit without incurring unlimited liability.*

*...Accordingly, in order to make it just to order a director to pay the costs of unsuccessful company litigation, it is necessary to show something more. This might be, for example, that the claim is not made in good faith, or for the benefit of the company, or it might be that the claim has been improperly conducted by the director."*[120]

<u>*Insolvent Companies*</u>

In the case of insolvent companies, a non-party's funding of the litigation may be particularly relevant in determining their motivation, but the extent to which they are "the real party" remains the primary consideration. In *Dymocks Franchise Systems (NSW) Pty Ltd v Todd* [2004] 1 WLR 2807 Lord Brown suggested that cases in which non-parties fund receivers, liquidators or financially insecure companies generally would be among the most difficult:

*"...their Lordships would hold that, generally speaking, where a non-party promotes and funds proceedings by an insolvent company solely or substantially for his own financial benefit, he should be liable for the costs if his claim or defence or appeal fails. As explained in the cases, however, that is not to say that orders will invariably be made in such cases, particularly, say, where the non-party is himself a director or liquidator who can realistically be regarded as*

[120] *Housemaker Services Ltd v Cole* [2017] EWHC 924 (Ch), at paragraph 15 per Judge Paul Matthews (Sitting as a Judge of the High Court).

> *acting rather in the interests of the company (and more especially its shareholders and creditors) than in his own interests."*[121]

In each case, therefore, the court will undertake an assessment of the reasons why the insolvent company has been put in funds, focusing on the funder's and the company's interest in litigating.

*Piercing the Corporate Veil?*

It is sometimes argued that the operative concept of "the real party" should not apply in the context of companies as it impermissibly fails to treat the company as having a distinct legal personality: it "pierces the corporate veil". The courts have however, been eager to stress that the company's discrete legal personality does not restrict the exercise of the court's discretion.

In *Threlfall v ECD Insight Ltd and another* [2013] EWCA Civ 1444 Lewison LJ addressed that argument directly:

> *"If a non-party costs order is made against a company director, it is quite wrong to characterise it as piercing or lifting the corporate veil… the separate personality of a corporation, even a single-member corporation, is deeply embedded in our law. But its purpose is to deal with legal rights and obligations. By contrast, the exercise of discretion to make a non-party costs order leaves rights and obligations where they are. The very fact that the making of such an order is discretionary demonstrates that the question is not one of rights and obligations of a non-party, for no obligations exist unless and until the court exercises its discretion… in deciding whether or not to make such an order, the court is not fettered by the legal realities. It is entitled to look to the economic realities. It is in this sense that*

[121] *Dymocks Franchise Systems (NSW) Pty Ltd v Todd* [2004] 1 WLR 2807, at paragraph 29 per Lord Brown.

> *many of the cases pose the question whether the non-party is 'the real party' in the case."*[122]

This commentary echoes what is evident in the general approach to the court's discretion on non-party costs orders (see Part 1): that the court is simply concerned with ensuring that the costs of litigation are ultimately met by the appropriate person, notwithstanding their procedural position.

[122] *Threlfall v ECD Insight Ltd and another* [2013] EWCA Civ 1444, at paragraph 13 per Lewison LJ.

# CHAPTER EIGHT
# LITIGATION FRIENDS

The court's approach to making a non-party costs order against a litigation friend will, it seems, differ depending on whether the litigation friend is that of a claimant or defendant.

The Civil Procedure Rules 1998 ('CPR') introduced the concept of a litigation friend. CPR 21.2 provides that a "protected party" – that is a party, or intended party, who lacks capacity to conduct the proceedings[123] – must have a litigation friend to conduct proceedings on his behalf. A child must have a litigation friend unless the court orders otherwise under CPR 21.2(3).

The CPR set out the conditions that must be satisfied for a person to become a litigation friend either by a court order (CPR 21.6 – 21.8) or without a court order (CPR 21.4 – 21.5).

<u>*Claimant's Litigation Friend*</u>

In practice, the court may not often need to consider whether to make a non-party costs order against a claimant's litigation friend.

With respect to a person who becomes a litigation friend without a court order, CPR 21.4(3)(c) provides:

> *21.4*
>
> …
>
> *(3) If nobody has been appointed by the court… a person may act as a litigation friend if he –*

---

[123] CPR 21.1(2)(d)

...

> *(c) where the child or protected party is a claimant, undertakes to pay any costs which the child or protected party may be ordered to pay in relation to the proceedings, subject to any right he may have to be repaid from the assets of the child or protected party.*

Likewise, with respect to a person whom the court appoints as a litigation friend, CPR 21.6(5) provides:

> *21.6*
>
> *(5) The court may not appoint a litigation friend under this rule unless it is satisfied that the person to be appointed satisfies the conditions in rule 21.4(3).*

A claimant's litigation friend will therefore often be responsible for any costs ordered against the claimant by virtue of their undertaking without the need for a non-party costs order. The question of non-party costs orders against a claimant's litigation friend is therefore only practically relevant when the claim fails but the court does not order the claimant to pay any costs (and therefore the CPR 21.4(3)(c) undertaking does not bite).

The Court of Appeal has recently considered this situation in *Barker v Confiance Ltd and others* [2020] EWCA Civ 1112 where Newey LJ said:

> *"it will usually be appropriate to make such an order if an order would have been made against the claimant himself had he not*

*been a child or protected party. That would reflect both the sense of CPR 21.4(3)(c) and pre-CPR authority."*[124]

However, that guidance should not be taken to curtail the court's discretion and is merely a general rule of thumb, as the court further noted:

> *"It remains the case that liability for costs should typically be imposed on a claimant's litigation friend, but with the important caveat that, when deciding whether to make such an order, the Court is exercising a discretion and entitled to have regard to the particular circumstances of the case."*[125]

Therefore, defendants who are denied a costs order against a claimant who is a protected party with a litigation friend should, in the first instance, look to the reasons behind that order when considering an application for a non-party costs order against the litigation friend.

<u>*Defendant's Litigation Friend*</u>

The position of a defendant's litigation friend is different. The court in *Barker* said, in response to an argument that the defendant's litigation friend should be treated in the same way as that of the claimant:

> *"There is no presumption that a defendant's litigation friend should bear costs which the defendant would have been ordered to pay if not a child or protected party. That the litigation friend controlled the defence of a claim which succeeded will not of itself generally*

[124] *Barker v Confiance Ltd and others* [2020] EWCA Civ 1112, at paragraph 62 per Newey LJ.

[125] *Barker v Confiance Ltd and others* [2020] EWCA Civ 1112, at paragraph 62 per Newey LJ.

> *make it just to make an adverse costs order against the litigation friend."*[126]

The court in *Barker* continued to set out factors relevant to the exercise of the discretion:

> *"Factors that might, depending on the specific facts, be thought to justify such an order include bad faith, improper or unreasonable behaviour and prospect of personal benefit. If a director causes his company to litigate 'solely or substantially for his own benefit' (to quote Lord Brown in Dymocks), that may point towards a costs order against him. The fact that a litigation friend stands to gain a substantial personal benefit must also, I think, be capable of weighing in favour of a costs order against him."*[127]

The court in *Barker* reiterated that the ultimate question will be whether it is just to make the order. However it seems that, in assessing the potential liability of a defendant's litigation friend for a non-party costs order, it will be necessary to look to whether he can be said to have become "the real party" or "a real party" by reason of his personal interest in the matter – as with company director cases (see Chapter 7).

Where it can be said that both the protected party and the litigation friend stand to benefit, it is suggested – by analogy with limits of cover insurance cases (see Chapter 4) – that it will be relevant to consider whether the litigation friend has allowed his interests to predominate over that of the protected party.

---

[126] *Barker v Confiance Ltd and others* [2020] EWCA Civ 1112, at paragraph 64 per Newey LJ.

[127] *Barker v Confiance Ltd and others* [2020] EWCA Civ 1112, at paragraph 64 per Newey LJ.

Finally, the non-party liability of litigation friends could be a further area where the intermeddling principle may be usefully developed in future cases. That is to say it may be relevant to ask whether a litigation friend has acted beyond his proper role and thereby intermeddled in the litigation, causing excess costs to be incurred. This, however, remains to be confirmed.

# CHAPTER NINE
# SOLICITORS

The case of *Tolstoy-Miloslavsky v Aldington* [1996] 1 WLR 736 provides a useful starting point for discussing the vulnerability of solicitors to non-party costs orders. In that case, Rose LJ said:

> *"there are only three categories of conduct which can give rise to an order for costs against a solicitor:*
>
> *(i) if it is within the wasted costs jurisdiction of section 51(6) and (7);*
> *(ii) if it is otherwise a breach of duty to the court such as, even before the Judicature Acts, could found an order, e.g., if he acts, even unwittingly, without authority or in breach of an undertaking;*
> *(iii) if he acts outside the role of solicitor, e.g., in a private capacity or as a true third-party funder for someone else."*[128]

In that case, the Court of Appeal did not consider that the non-party costs jurisdiction would be applicable to solicitors. However, when the subsequent case of *Myatt v National Coal Board and another (No 2)* [2007] 1 WLR 1559 came before the same court some ten years later, Dyson LJ said:

> *"In my judgment, the third category described by Rose LJ in the Tolstoy-Miloslavsky case should be understood as including a solicitor who, to use the words of Lord Brown in Dymocks Franchise Systems (NSW) Pty Ltd v Todd is 'a real party... in very important and critical respects' and who 'not merely funds the proceedings but*

[128] *Tolstoy-Miloslavsky v Aldington* [1996] 1 WLR 736, at 745-6 per Rose LJ.

> *substantially also controls or at any rate is to benefit from them'. I do not accept that the mere fact that a solicitor is on the record prosecuting proceedings for his or her client is fatal to an application by the successful opposing party under section 51(1) and (3) of the Supreme Court Act 1981, that the solicitor should pay some or all of the costs."*[129]

The relevant practical consideration, therefore, for understanding a solicitor's potential liability under a non-party costs order is when they will be found to have acted outside their proper role.[130]

In light of the legislation and the well-known professional standards regulating solicitors' professional conduct, in most cases, it should be relatively clear when a solicitor will be acting beyond their proper role – including acting in a "private capacity" per Rose LJ, above.

Another example offered by Rose LJ in *Tolstoy-Miloslavsky v Aldington* [1996] 1 WLR 736 of when solicitors may be found to have acted outside their role is when they are a "true third-party funder".

*A "True Third-Party Funder"*

The fact that liability can be imposed when a solicitor acts as a "true third-party funder" reflects the importance of funding in the general principles concerning "the real party" or "a real party" discussed in Chapters 2 and 3.

---

[129] *Myatt v National Coal Board and another (No 2)* [2007] 1 WLR 1559 – *Though the substantive decision in Myatt was reversed in the Supreme Court, the reasoning of Dyson LJ on this point was not disturbed and has been subsequently cited with approval: see Flatman v Germany (Law Society intervening); Weddall v Barchester Health Care Ltd (Same intervening)* [2013] 1 WLR 2676.

[130] It is noteworthy and relatively unsurprising, given the state of the caselaw at the time of the relevant appeals, that the court has analysed this area in terms of the "a real party" principle so far; it may be, in light of *Travelers*, that the intermeddling principle falls to be applied in this area in future decisions.

It is perfectly common, and even normal, that a solicitor will – in the first place – pay the up-front costs incurred during the course of litigation and invoice the client thereafter. A solicitor may thereby be said to be extending credit, or even providing funding, to the client. However, it is settled law that this will not constitute acting outside the role of a solicitor and render them vulnerable to a non-party costs order.[131] It is similarly settled that solicitors are entitled to act for an impecunious client whom they know, or suspect, will not be able to pay their own (or the other side's costs), if unsuccessful.[132]

In reasoning subsequently approved by the Court of Appeal, Eady J in *Germany v Flatman* [2011] EWHC 2945 (QB) indicated that a certain degree of benefit accruing to the solicitor in this context may be sufficient:

> *"It may suffice, depending upon the circumstances, that the funder has something to gain alongside the nominal party. In the case of a solicitor, for example, it is not necessary to demonstrate that in the event of the litigation leading to a successful outcome he would be the sole beneficiary. Even though his client may recover compensation for himself, the solicitor could still be regarded as benefiting, or potentially benefiting, from the case to the extent that a costs order should be made against him."*[133]

This does no more than reflect Lord Brown's description of "the real party" in *Dymocks Franchise Systems (NSW) Pty Ltd v Todd* [2004] 1 WLR 2807, as a "non-party [who] not merely funds the proceedings

[131] See *Floods of Queensferry Ltd v Shand Construction Ltd* [2002] EWCA Civ 918, at paragraph 85 per Hale LJ.

[132] Ibid and see also *Sibthorpe v Southwark London Borough Council (Law Society intervening)* [2011] 1 WLR 2111, at 2125 per Lord Neuberger MR; *Awwad v Geraghty & Co* [2001] QB 570, at 588 per Schiemann LJ.

[133] *Germany v Flatman* [2011] EWHC 2945 (QB), at paragraph 16 per Eady J.

but substantially also controls or at any rate is to benefit from them".[134] The issue of benefit becomes more finely balanced in the context of certain conditional fee agreements ('CFA') which have been considered by the courts.

## *Conditional Fee Agreements*

Section 58 of the Courts and Legal Services Act 1990 makes CFAs lawful. A CFA is defined by section 58(2)(a) as:

> *"an agreement with a person providing advocacy or litigation services which provides for his fees and expenses or any part of them to be payable only in specified circumstances".*

CFAs can also attract "success fees", that is to say an uplift on the solicitor's base fees should the litigation be successful. A solicitor acting under CFA with a success fee, and who extends credit to an impecunious client, therefore seems to satisfy both the funding and the benefit element of this description. Would such an arrangement expose the solicitor to the possibility of a non-party costs order?

Such an arrangement appears to come well within the ambit of Lord Brown's dictum.[135] Nevertheless, it seems the answer is that, provided the agreement comes within the meaning of section 58 of the 1990 Act, it would not be "outside the role of a solicitor".

The applicants in *Germany* argued (in part) that the non-party solicitors, who had paid disbursements effectively in the hope of obtaining a success fee, should be liable for costs in a situation akin to that of a

---

[134] *Dymocks Franchise Systems (NSW) Pty Ltd v Todd* [2004] 1 WLR 2807, at paragraph 25 per Lord Brown.

[135] *Dymocks Franchise Systems (NSW) Pty Ltd v Todd* [2004] 1 WLR 2807, at paragraph 25 per Lord Brown.

commercial funder. They argued that the solicitors' payment of disbursements meant they could not benefit from the argument they were within the proper "role of the solicitor". The Court of Appeal[136] disagreed and held that the 1990 Act:

> *"does visualise the possibility that a solicitor might fund disbursements and, in that event, it would not be right to conclude that such a solicitor was 'the real party' or even 'a real party' to the litigation."*[137]

Coming within the ambit of the 1990 Act's terms therefore seems to bring a solicitor within Rose LJ's third category in *Tolstoy*. This appears to protect a solicitor who might otherwise be considered to be "the real party" or "a real party", applying the familiar dicta.

[136] In the Court of Appeal: *Flatman v Germany (Law Society intervening); Weddall v Barchester Health Care Ltd (Same intervening)* [2013] 1 WLR 2676.

[137] *Flatman v Germany (Law Society intervening); Weddall v Barchester Health Care Ltd (Same intervening)* [2013] 1 WLR 2676, at 2690 per Leveson LJ.

# CHAPTER TEN
# TRADE UNIONS

Although not the subject of recently reported cases, trade unions merit some consideration as they may be something of a special case with respect to non-party costs orders.

In the context of the general principles on non-party funders, trade unions appear to be akin to either insurers or even pure funders. That is to say the motivation for the trade union funding litigation will ordinarily be some form of obligation and/or the vindication of workers' rights the organisation exists to promote – not, strictly speaking, financial gain.

*Hill v Archbold* [1968] 1 QB 686 concerned the tort of maintenance in the context of litigation funded by a trade union. However, the case is relevant as regards the modern non-party costs jurisdiction as it evidences a convention that trade unions will normally be liable for costs of litigation they support. The question for the Court of Appeal was the lawfulness of a trade union meeting the legal costs of two union officials. Giving the leading judgment, Lord Denning explained the position not only in terms of officials but also members of the union:

> *"Most of the actions in our courts are supported by some association or other, or by the state itself. Comparatively few litigants bring suits, or defend them, at their own expense. Most claims by workmen against their employers are paid for by a trade union.... This is perfectly justifiable and is accepted by everyone as lawful, provided always that the one who supports the litigation, if it fails, pays the costs of the other side. It is the universal experience in this court that if a*

> *trade union or an insurance company supports a case and fails, it pays the costs of the other side."*[138]

It appears to be generally accepted that a trade union involved in funding litigation will bear some costs liability should the claim they support fail. This, notwithstanding the fact that the motivation for funding is seldom financial gain and it may therefore be said that a trade union uneasily fits within the concepts of "the real party" or "a real party" (see Chapter 2). Nevertheless, it may simply be that the benefit to the union of their member's litigation succeeding – as intangible as it may be – is a sufficient interest to attract the non-party costs jurisdiction, when taken together with historical convention.

This general conclusion was recognised in *Cooper v Maxwell* (unreported) 20 March 1992; Court of Appeal (Civil Division) Transcript No 273 of 1992, in which Dillon LJ observed:

> *"The development of the authorities has not been that there will automatically be an order for costs against a person who is not a party to the proceedings if that person has funded the litigation. More is required. It is not suggested that a bank which funded litigation by providing an overdraft for a party to litigation on commercial terms would automatically be ordered to pay the other side's costs if the litigation was unsuccessful. The position could be different with a trade union which has an interest in funding the litigation of a member in the industrial field and habitually does pay the costs if the litigation fails."*[139]

In *Condliffe v Hislop* [1996] 1 WLR 753 the Court of Appeal analogised the trade union relationship with that of an insurer or a

[138] *Hill v Archbold* [1968] 1 QB 686, at 695 per Lord Denning.

[139] Cited in *Hamilton v Al Fayed (No 2)* [2002] EWCA Civ 665, at paragraph 24 per Simon Brown LJ.

commercial litigation funder as those arising in "a business context". The court in that case endorsed the approach taken by Longmore J in *McFarlane v EE Caledonia Ltd (No 2)* [1995] 1 WLR 366 where a non-party costs order was made on the finding of such a relationship, which would be a "highly relevant consideration". It is to be noted however that the concept of benefit accruing in "a business context" has not been widely employed in subsequent cases.

Although not a case concerning trade unions, the clearest annunciation of the principles applicable to trade unions comes from Phillips LJ in *Murphy v Young & Co.'s Brewery Plc.* [1997] 1 WLR 1591 as part of a dictum tracing the interaction with the old law on maintenance and champerty and the modern non-party costs jurisdiction:

> *"Where a trade union funds unsuccessful litigation on behalf of a member the following factors, in addition to the funding itself, are likely to be present and, where they are, to make it appropriate to order the union to pay the successful party's costs should such an order be necessary:*
>
> *(a) an implied obligation owed by the union to its member to do so...;*
>
> *(b) an interest on the part of the union in supporting and being seen to support the member's claim;*
>
> *(c) the conduct of the litigation;*
>
> *(d) expectation based on convention that the union will bear the costs of the successful party should the member lose."*[140]

It appears therefore that the interest that a trade union has in the success of its members' litigation it funds – together with the expectation

---

[140] *Murphy v Young & Co.'s Brewery Plc.* [1997] 1 WLR 1591, at 1601 per Phillips LJ.

evident from the dicta cited above – is sufficient to establish a connection that engages the modern non-party costs jurisdiction.

# PART THREE
# PROCEDURE

In *Aiden Shipping Co Ltd v Interbulk Ltd (The Vimeira) (No 2)* [1986] AC 965, Lord Goff suggested that the Rules Committee may become involved in regulating the non-party costs jurisdiction.[141] Rule 46.2 of the Civil Procedure Rules 1998 ('CPR') provides:

> *46.2*
>
> *(1) Where the court is considering whether to exercise its power under section 51 of the Senior Courts Act 1981 (costs are in the discretion of the court) to make a costs order in favour of or against a person who is not a party to proceedings, that person must –*
> *(a) be added as a party to the proceedings for the purposes of costs only; and*
> *(b) be given a reasonable opportunity to attend a hearing at which the court will consider the matter further.*
>
> *(2) This rule does not apply –*
> *(a) where the court is considering whether to –*
> *(i) make an order against the Lord Chancellor in proceedings in which the Lord Chancellor has provided legal aid to a party to the proceedings;*
> *(ii) make a wasted costs order (as defined in rule 46.8); and*
> *(b) in proceedings to which rule 46.1 applies (pre-commencement disclosure and orders for disclosure against a person who is not a party).*

---

[141] *Aiden Shipping Co Ltd v Interbulk Ltd (The Vimeira) (No 2)* [1986] AC 965, at 981 per Lord Goff.

Beyond this rule, however, the CPR does not provide much further assistance, in setting out the procedural steps to be taken in pursuing a non-party costs order. Practice Direction 46 is silent on the matter. Much like the principles affecting the exercise of the discretion, therefore, it has fallen to courts to elaborate on the relevant procedure. This part will focus on that procedural guidance.

# CHAPTER ELEVEN
# PROCEDURE, ANCILLARY ORDERS AND APPEALS

Practitioners will be familiar with the procedural considerations that apply to the making of applications in civil litigation generally.[142] This chapter will not reiterate that familiar general guidance but will focus on those elements that are particularly relevant in the context of non-party costs orders.

## Notice

As discussed earlier,[143] and although there is no formal notice requirement, it is wise to put the non-party on notice that an application for a non-party costs order will be made as soon as possible. A failure to do so may be relevant in the determination of the application.

## The Application

A non-party costs order is "supplemental to the judgment";[144] it can therefore be obtained before[145] costs have been assessed or after a judgment providing for an *inter partes* costs order has been sealed.

The application itself should set out the matters relied upon, seek permission to have the non-party added for the purposes of costs and

[142] See, for example, CPR 23 and associated practice directions.

[143] See Chapter 3.

[144] *Dymocks Franchise Systems (NSW) Pty Ltd v Todd* [2004] 1 WLR 2807, at paragraph 17 per Lord Brown.

[145] *See Loson and another v Stack and another* [2016] EWCA Civ 610, at paragraphs 19 – 21 per Jackson LJ.

propose directions for the substantive hearing. The application should be served on all the other parties to the action.[146]

At the stage of considering the joinder of the non-party, that application should be acceded to unless it could be said that the application was an abuse of process. It is not necessary for the applicant to show that he has an arguable case at the joinder stage.[147] CPR 46.2(1) gives the erstwhile non-party the right to be heard at the substantive hearing thereafter.

The application should be made to the trial judge.[148] It has been said that:

> *"The application should normally be determined by the trial judge who could give effect to any views he had expressed as to the conduct of the non-party without constituting bias or the appearance of bias."*[149]

The involvement of the trial judge has been justified by the Court of Appeal in *Deutsche Bank A.G. v Sebastian Holdings Inc. and Alexander Vik* [2016] EWCA Civ 23:

---

[146] *National Justice Compania Naviera SA v Prudential Assurance Co Ltd; The Ikarian Reefer* [2000] 1 All ER 37, at 47 per Waller LJ.

[147] See *PR Records Ltd v Vinyl 2000 Ltd and another* [2007] EWHC 1721 (Ch), per Morgan J.

[148] See *Bahai v Rashidian* [1985] 1 WLR 1337, cited in *Symphony Group Plc. v Hodgson* [1994] QB 179, at 193 per Balcombe LJ.

[149] *Thomson v Berkhamsted Collegiate School* [2009] EWHC 2374 (QB), at paragraph 18 per Blake J – endorsed by the Court of Appeal in *Flatman v Germany (Law Society intervening); Weddall v Barchester Health Care Ltd (Same intervening)* [2013] 1 WLR 2676, at 2691 per Leveson LJ. See also *Symphony Group Plc. v Hodgson* [1994] QB 179, at 193 per Balcombe LJ.

> *"It is necessary for these purposes to assume that the judge has conducted the trial impartially and that, if he has made findings critical of the third party, those findings were justified. Making findings of fact is part of the judicial function and to have made findings critical of one party or another does not disable the judge from dealing with consequential matters impartially, even when they turn on facts in respect of which he has already made findings.... Accordingly, although we would not wish to exclude altogether the possibility that there may be cases in which an application of that kind should be decided by someone other than the trial judge, such cases are likely to be rare."*[150]

In practice, there have been few exceptions[151] to the principle that the trial judge should hear the application.

*The Determination*

The court's discretion on non-party costs extends to the form of order to be made, the proportion of any costs to be paid, the basis[152] and the quantum of (including interest upon)[153] any award.[154] It is not a requirement that, if costs have already been assessed, they need to be reassessed if a non-party costs order is subsequently made. Nor, if a

[150] *Deutsche Bank A.G. v Sebastian Holdings Inc. and Alexander Vik* [2016] EWCA Civ 23, at paragraph 58 per Moore-Bick LJ.

[151] See *Goknur Gida Maddeleri Enerji Imalat Ithalat Ihracat Ticaret Ve Sanati AS v Organic Village Ltd and another* [2020] EWHC 2542 (QB), at paragraphs 9 – 13 per Matthew Gullick (sitting as a deputy judge of the High Court).

[152] See *Excalibur Ventures LLC v Texas Keystone Inc. and others* [2016] EWCA Civ 1144.

[153] See *Sony/ATV Music Publishing LLC and another company v WPMC Ltd (in liquidation) and others* [2017] EWHC 456 (Ch).

[154] See *Nelson v Greening* [2007] EWCA Civ 1358, at paragraph 62 per Lawrence Collins LJ; and *ChapelGate Credit Opportunity Master Fund Limited v Money and others* [2020] EWCA Civ 246.

non-party costs order is made, it does not have to be on the basis of joint and several liability with the litigant.

The court is restricted to awarding (per section 51(1) of the Senior Courts Act 1981) "the costs of and incidental to all proceedings..." This was clarified by Aldous LJ in *Zanussi v Anglos Venezuelan Real Estate and Agricultural Development Limited* (The Times, 18th April 1996 CA) who confirmed that a non-party cannot be made liable to a greater extent than a litigant could be:

> *"In my view the word 'all' in s51 means 'in every proceeding which is before the court'. I conclude that s51 does not confer a jurisdiction upon a court to award costs, other than costs incurred in the proceedings before the court or incidental to those proceedings."*[155]

Non-parties will not automatically be bound by the findings of the trial judge. It is clear from the reasoning of the Court of Appeal in in *Deutsche Bank* that the question as to whether non-parties should be bound by findings in the main action forms part of the exercise of the discretion, at least when applying concepts such as "the real party" or "a real party".[156] As regards intermeddling, it will often be necessary for the court to establish the facts pertinent to the intermeddling after the joinder of the non-party where, of course, it will benefit from all the usual procedural protections.

The determination of the application for a non-party costs order is to be summary in nature *"in the sense that the judge would make an order*

[155] *Zanussi v Anglos Venezuelan Real Estate and Agricultural Development Limited* (The Times, 18th April 1996 CA), at paragraph 110 per Aldous LJ.

[156] *Deutsche Bank A.G. v Sebastian Holdings Inc. and Alexander Vik* [2016] EWCA Civ 23, at paragraph 17 per Moore-Bick LJ; *Symphony Group Plc. v Hodgson* [1994] QB 179, at 193 per Balcombe LJ.

*based on the evidence given and the facts found at trial, together with his assessment of the behaviour of those involved in the proceedings."*[157]

In *Global Equities Ltd v Globe Legal Services Ltd* [1999] All ER (D) 226, Morritt LJ said:

> *"it must be borne in mind that this court has said on more than one occasion that proceedings in respect of orders such as these [which included an application for a non-party costs order] should be dealt with in a summary way, to be measured in hours not days, and not allowed to give rise to substantial satellite litigation: Ridehalgh v Horsefield [1994] Ch 205, 238."*[158]

This does not mean that the court is incapable of dealing with complex cases, however it must act proportionately. In *Deepchand and another v Sooben* [2020] EWCA Civ 1409 Arnold LJ summarised:

> *"An application for a non-party costs order... should only be made if it can be determined proportionately by means of a summary procedure... If the application cannot be determined proportionately, then it should not be made."*[159]

Where appropriate, the court will make ancillary orders.[160] Often, for example, an order for further disclosure is sought as to the identity of

157 *Deutsche Bank A.G. v Sebastian Holdings Inc. and Alexander Vik* [2016] EWCA Civ 23, at paragraph 17 per Moore-Bick LJ.

158 *Global Equities Ltd v Globe Legal Services Ltd* [1999] All ER (D) 226, at paragraph 3 per Morritt LJ.

159 *Deepchand and another v Sooben* [2020] EWCA Civ 1409, at paragraph 35 per Arnold LJ. This also echoes the requirements of the overriding objective (see CPR 1.1 and 1.2).

160 See *Flatman v Germany (Law Society intervening); Weddall v Barchester Health Care Ltd (Same intervening)* [2013] 1 WLR 2676, at 2691 – 2691 per Leveson LJ.

funders. Absent statutory guidance, the court may have to be somewhat more prescriptive in setting down directions.

*Ancillary Orders*

When seeking a non-party costs order that may necessitate the making of ancillary orders, such as for disclosure, inspection or cross-examination, it is wise to be mindful that CPR 46.2 is intended to be a summary procedure.

The inherent strength of the application and the sums involved will be relevant factors in determining applications for ancillary orders. This was explained by Blake J in *Thomson v Berkhamsted Collegiate School* [2009] EWHC 2374 (QB) in a dictum later endorsed by the Court of Appeal:[161]

> *"In determining these applications the court must exercise its case management powers to ensure that the application does not turn into satellite litigation that results in prolonged, complex and over-extended arguments about costs about costs. For that reason the inherent strength of the application is always a relevant factor."*[162]

On the specific question of whether an order for disclosure is necessary and proportionate for the fair determination of the application, the relevant factors were set out by Blake J in *Thomson* as:

> *"(i) the strength of the application as it now appears unassisted by disclosure;*

[161] *Flatman v Germany (Law Society intervening); Weddall v Barchester Health Care Ltd (Same intervening)* [2013] 1 WLR 2676, at 2691 per Leveson LJ

[162] *Thomson v Berkhamsted Collegiate School* [2009] EWHC 2374 (QB), at paragraph 18 per Blake J.

*(ii) the potential value to the fair determination of the application of the documents of which the claimant seeks disclosure and whether they are likely to elucidate considerations highly probative of the exercise of the court's discretion, or threaten to drag the application into a side alley of satellite litigation with diminishing returns for the overall issue;*

*(iii) whether on a summary assessment it is obvious that the documents for which disclosure is sought will be the subject of proper legal professional privilege;*

*(iv) whether the likely effect of any order the court might be minded to make will be proportionate and just in all the circumstances."*[163]

<u>*Appealing a Non-Party Costs Order*</u>

In *Floods of Queensferry Ltd and another v Shand Construction Ltd and others* [2002] EWCA Civ 918, Buxton LJ said:

> *"the decision under s 51 is a discretionary decision for the trial judge. The normal diffidence this court has in interfering with a discretionary decision will apply to it."*[164]

An aggrieved party may appeal a non-party costs order in the normal way. However, the discretionary nature of the jurisdiction means that an appellate court will only consider whether the judge at first instance

163 *Thomson v Berkhamsted Collegiate School* [2009] EWHC 2374 (QB), at paragraph 18 per Blake J.

164 *Floods of Queensferry Ltd and another v Shand Construction Ltd and others* [2002] EWCA Civ 918, at paragraph 18 per Buxton LJ.

"erred in principle or reached a decision outside the generous range of reasonable decisions open to him."[165]

In *G v G (Minors: Custody Appeal)* [1985] 1 WLR 647, Lord Fraser set out that appeal judges:

> *"should only interfere when they consider that the judge of first instance has not merely preferred an imperfect solution which is different from an alternative imperfect solution which the Court of Appeal might or would have adopted, but has exceeded the generous ambit within which a reasonable disagreement is possible".*[166]

This approach is illustrated by Tomlinson LJ's summary in *Excalibur Ventures LLC v Texas Keystone Inc. and others* [2016] EWCA Civ 1144 where, dismissing the appeal, he found the judge of first instance:

> "*exercise[d] this discretion in a principled manner, not taking into account irrelevant factors and not omitting to take into account relevant factors. He reached a conclusion which was not just within the ambit of reasonable decision-making but which was plainly and obviously just, correct and appropriate. There is no basis upon which this court could or should interfere.*"[167]

In practice, therefore, it seems it will generally be difficult for aggrieved applicants for, or subjects of, a non-party costs order to disturb a first instance determination on appeal.

---

[165] *Turvill v Bird and Others* [2016] EWCA Civ 703, at paragraph 29 per Hamblen LJ.

[166] *G v G (Minors: Custody Appeal)* [1985] 1 WLR 647, at 652 per Lord Fraser.

[167] *Excalibur Ventures LLC v Texas Keystone Inc. and others* [2016] EWCA Civ 1144, at paragraph 52 per Tomlinson LJ

# MORE BOOKS BY LAW BRIEF PUBLISHING

A selection of our other titles available now:-

| |
|---|
| 'Covid-19, Homeworking and the Law – The Essential Guide to Employment and GDPR Issues' by Forbes Solicitors |
| 'Covid-19, Force Majeure and Frustration of Contracts – The Essential Guide' by Keith Markham |
| 'Covid-19 and Criminal Law – The Essential Guide' by Ramya Nagesh |
| 'Covid-19 and Family Law in England and Wales – The Essential Guide' by Safda Mahmood |
| 'Covid-19 and the Implications for Planning Law – The Essential Guide' by Bob Mc Geady & Meyric Lewis |
| 'Covid-19, Residential Property, Equity Release and Enfranchisement – The Essential Guide' by Paul Sams and Louise Uphill |
| 'Covid-19, Brexit and the Law of Commercial Leases – The Essential Guide' by Mark Shelton |
| 'Covid-19 and the Law Relating to Food in the UK and Republic of Ireland – The Essential Guide' by Ian Thomas |
| 'A Practical Guide to the General Data Protection Regulation (GDPR) – 2nd Edition' by Keith Markham |
| 'Ellis on Credit Hire – Sixth Edition' by Aidan Ellis & Tim Kevan |
| 'A Practical Guide to Working with Litigants in Person and McKenzie Friends in Family Cases' by Stuart Barlow |
| 'Protecting Unregistered Brands: A Practical Guide to the Law of Passing Off' by Lorna Brazell |
| 'A Practical Guide to Secondary Liability and Joint Enterprise Post-Jogee' by Joanne Cecil & James Mehigan |

| |
|---|
| 'A Practical Guide to the Pre-Action RTA Claims Protocol for Personal Injury Lawyers' by Antonia Ford |
| 'A Practical Guide to Neighbour Disputes and the Law' by Alexander Walsh |
| 'A Practical Guide to Forfeiture of Leases' by Mark Shelton |
| 'A Practical Guide to Coercive Control for Legal Practitioners and Victims' by Rachel Horman |
| 'A Practical Guide to Rights Over Airspace and Subsoil' by Daniel Gatty |
| 'Tackling Disclosure in the Criminal Courts – A Practitioner's Guide' by Narita Bahra QC & Don Ramble |
| 'A Practical Guide to the Law of Driverless Cars – Second Edition' by Alex Glassbrook, Emma Northey & Scarlett Milligan |
| 'A Practical Guide to TOLATA Claims' by Greg Williams |
| 'Artificial Intelligence – The Practical Legal Issues' by John Buyers |
| 'A Practical Guide to the Law of Prescription in Scotland' by Andrew Foyle |
| 'A Practical Guide to the Construction and Rectification of Wills and Trust Instruments' by Edward Hewitt |
| 'A Practical Guide to the Law of Bullying and Harassment in the Workplace' by Philip Hyland |
| 'How to Be a Freelance Solicitor: A Practical Guide to the SRA-Regulated Freelance Solicitor Model' by Paul Bennett |
| 'A Practical Guide to Prison Injury Claims' by Malcolm Johnson |
| 'A Practical Guide to the Small Claims Track' by Dominic Bright |
| 'A Practical Guide to Advising Clients at the Police Station' by Colin Stephen McKeown-Beaumont |
| 'A Practical Guide to Antisocial Behaviour Injunctions' by Iain Wightwick |
| 'Practical Mediation: A Guide for Mediators, Advocates, Advisers, Lawyers, and Students in Civil, Commercial, Business, Property, Workplace, and Employment Cases' by Jonathan Dingle with John Sephton |
| 'The Mini-Pupillage Workbook' by David Boyle |

| |
|---|
| 'A Practical Guide to Crofting Law' by Brian Inkster |
| 'A Practical Guide to Spousal Maintenance' by Liz Cowell |
| 'A Practical Guide to the Law of Domain Names and Cybersquatting' by Andrew Clemson |
| 'A Practical Guide to the Law of Gender Pay Gap Reporting' by Harini Iyengar |
| 'A Practical Guide to the Rights of Grandparents in Children Proceedings' by Stuart Barlow |
| 'NHS Whistleblowing and the Law' by Joseph England |
| 'Employment Law and the Gig Economy' by Nigel Mackay & Annie Powell |
| 'A Practical Guide to Noise Induced Hearing Loss (NIHL) Claims' by Andrew Mckie, Ian Skeate, Gareth McAloon |
| 'An Introduction to Beauty Negligence Claims – A Practical Guide for the Personal Injury Practitioner' by Greg Almond |
| 'Intercompany Agreements for Transfer Pricing Compliance' by Paul Sutton |
| 'Zen and the Art of Mediation' by Martin Plowman |
| 'A Practical Guide to the SRA Principles, Individual and Law Firm Codes of Conduct 2019 – What Every Law Firm Needs to Know' by Paul Bennett |
| 'A Practical Guide to Adoption for Family Lawyers' by Graham Pegg |
| 'A Practical Guide to Industrial Disease Claims' by Andrew Mckie & Ian Skeate |
| 'A Practical Guide to Redundancy' by Philip Hyland |
| 'A Practical Guide to Vicarious Liability' by Mariel Irvine |
| 'A Practical Guide to Applications for Landlord's Consent and Variation of Leases' by Mark Shelton |
| 'A Practical Guide to Relief from Sanctions Post-Mitchell and Denton' by Peter Causton |
| 'A Practical Guide to Equity Release for Advisors' by Paul Sams |
| 'A Practical Guide to Unlawful Eviction and Harassment' by Stephanie Lovegrove |
| 'A Practical Guide to the Law Relating to Food' by Ian Thomas |

| |
|---|
| 'A Practical Guide to Financial Services Claims' by Chris Hegarty |
| 'The Law of Houses in Multiple Occupation: A Practical Guide to HMO Proceedings' by Julian Hunt |
| 'A Practical Guide to Unlawful Eviction and Harassment' by Stephanie Lovegrove |
| 'A Practical Guide to Solicitor and Client Costs' by Robin Dunne |
| 'Occupiers, Highways and Defective Premises Claims: A Practical Guide Post-Jackson – 2nd Edition' by Andrew Mckie |
| 'A Practical Guide to Financial Ombudsman Service Claims' by Adam Temple & Robert Scrivenor |
| 'A Practical Guide to Advising Schools on Employment Law' by Jonathan Holden |
| 'A Practical Guide to Running Housing Disrepair and Cavity Wall Claims: 2nd Edition' by Andrew Mckie & Ian Skeate |
| 'A Practical Guide to Holiday Sickness Claims – 2nd Edition' by Andrew Mckie & Ian Skeate |
| 'Arguments and Tactics for Personal Injury and Clinical Negligence Claims' by Dorian Williams |
| 'A Practical Guide to QOCS and Fundamental Dishonesty' by James Bentley |
| 'A Practical Guide to Drone Law' by Rufus Ballaster, Andrew Firman, Eleanor Clot |
| 'A Practical Guide to Compliance for Personal Injury Firms Working With Claims Management Companies' by Paul Bennett |
| 'A Practical Guide to the Landlord and Tenant Act 1954: Commercial Tenancies' by Richard Hayes & David Sawtell |
| 'A Practical Guide to Dog Law for Owners and Others' by Andrea Pitt |
| 'RTA Allegations of Fraud in a Post-Jackson Era: The Handbook – 2nd Edition' by Andrew Mckie |
| 'RTA Personal Injury Claims: A Practical Guide Post-Jackson' by Andrew Mckie |
| 'On Experts: CPR35 for Lawyers and Experts' by David Boyle |
| 'An Introduction to Personal Injury Law' by David Boyle |

www.ingramcontent.com/pod-product-compliance
Ingram Content Group UK Ltd.
Pitfield, Milton Keynes, MK11 3LW, UK
UKHW020149290926
15471UKWH00004B/778

9 781913 715564